Inclusion

Also by Eric H. F. Law,
published by Chalice Press

The Wolf Shall Dwell with the Lamb

The Bush Was Blazing But Not Consumed

Inclusion

Making Room for Grace

Eric H. F. Law

Chalice Press

St. Louis, Missouri

Cover art and design: Bob Watkins
Art direction: Elizabeth Wright
Interior design: Wynn Younker

This book is printed on acid-free, recycled paper.

Visit Chalice Press on the World Wide Web at
www.chalicepress.com

10 9 8 7 6 5 4 3   03 04 05

Library of Congress Cataloging–in–Publication Data

Law, Eric H. F.
    Inclusion : making room for grace / Eric H. F. Law.
        p.   cm.
    Includes bibliographical references.
    ISBN 0-8272-1620-3
    1. Christian life. 2. Conduct of life. 3. Faith. 4. God—Love. 5. Grace (Theology) 6. Salvation. I. Title.
BV4515.2 .L38 2000
261.8'34 — dc21   00-009352

Printed in the United States of America

For Gurdon Brewster,
my mentor, my priest,
who inspired me many years ago
to dedicate my life
to the ministry of inclusion

Contents

Acknowledgments

I am grateful for the invitation from the Richard and Alice Netter Labor-Management-Public Interest Seminar at Cornell University to give a lecture on the subject of "Inclusive Workplaces" in 1998. That experience planted the seed for this book. As I was working on this book, I found myself revisiting the many insights I gained studying with Walter Wink, whose Transforming Bible Study method is truly transforming. I give thanks for Frank Griswold, the Presiding Bishop of the Episcopal Church, for his wisdom and graciousness. I am indebted to Catherine Roskam, the Suffragan Bishop of the Episcopal Diocese of New York, for her enthusiastic support of me as a friend and of my work. I also appreciate the opportunities to work in more extensive ways with the congregations in her region. I thank Michael Ingham, Bishop of the Anglican Diocese of New Westminster, for inviting me to work in Canada and for allowing me to work with all the congregations in his diocese for three intriguing years. I thank David Polk, my editor, for his patience and understanding while the content and title of this book evolved over the year. I give thanks for Steve Rutberg for being a faithful companion through this journey. As always, I thank Kent Steinbrenner for reading the final draft of this book. Most of all, I am grateful to all the congregations from the various denominations that I worked with over the years in the United States and in Canada. Even though in the examples I gave in this book their identities were sufficiently disguised for the purpose of confidentiality, their willingness to allow me to walk with them in the grace margin is truly an experience of grace for me.

Introduction

Inclusion and diversity are words that are used frequently these days. Although much material justifies our being inclusive and appreciating diversity, there is a lack of resources and training in practical, theologically based approaches to enabling a community to act inclusively when its boundary is challenged. Church leaders, both experienced and new, often discover that good intention is not enough to create an inclusive community. This book seeks to fill this gap by providing practical and theologically sound theories, models, and skills that are necessary for moving a faith community toward greater inclusion.

In my previous two books, *The Wolf Shall Dwell with the Lamb* and *The Bush Was Blazing but Not Consumed,* I laid out the foundational skills, theories, and theologies from a leadership perspective for creating inclusive community. They include skills for bringing together people of diverse backgrounds and techniques required to create an environment that will not favor one group over another, but will support and affirm each group, enabling them to dialogue constructively for the purpose of building a stronger, more faithful community. Many of the techniques and processes named in this volume came from my last two books.

In this volume I focus on the process of inclusion from a community perspective. When I address the issue of inclusion this way, I am, in effect, speaking to the insiders of a community, especially to those who have leadership roles, power, and influence in the community. (Seeking to be included from an outsider's perspective is a different process, requiring a different set of analysis, skills, and theology that will require a separate volume to explore.) As I wrote on the subject, I discovered a lack of vocabulary and clarity in the way we use our language regarding inclusion. I found myself inventing new phrases like "boundary challenge," "boundary function," and "grace margin" to carry on this task of describing the process of inclusion. Readers might find these terms to be jargon, but the terms will have to do for now, since the English language does not provide too many useful vocabularies for our purpose. Also, we do not have a workable definition of the word *inclusion* used to consider people and community life. I would like to present my working definition of inclusion here. In chapter 4, I will explain how I arrived at this definition:

> Inclusion is a discipline of extending our boundary to take into consideration another's needs, interests, experience, and perspective, which will lead to clearer understanding of ourselves and others, fuller description of the issue at hand, and possibly a newly negotiated boundary of the community to which we belong.

Chapters 5 through 10 further explore and describe the inclusion process in Christian theological terms and practical facilitation skills and processes. At the end of each of these chapters are suggested techniques, processes, and programmatic strategies that can prepare a community to respond better to its boundary challenges. Although this book is intended to be an independent resource, I found it hard, especially in chapter 9, not to make references to the techniques, skills, and processes that I described in my previous two books. To gain a fuller and more in-depth reading of the later chapters, readers may want to read my previous two books first if they have not done so.

The central purpose of the process and model described in this book is to enable a community to extend its boundary to include an outsider's experience and perspective in a constructive and faithful way. This process is about transformation of a community from within, moving from being an exclusive community toward being a gracious, inclusive body of Christ. My hope is that you, the readers, will gain a sense of clarity and a practical approach to the discipline of inclusion. I pray that you will incorporate the theology that supports inclusion in your daily life and in communities in which you belong.

1

Now That Faith Has Come:
Resisting the Impulse to Exclude

When I started working on this book, I had difficulty focusing on the central topic: inclusion. Whenever I got close to
writing down an idea, my train of thought would be inter-
cepted by these questions: But what about _how_ we exclude?
How would I deal with all the justifications for exclusion coming from my readers? Immediately, I would think of the many
ways that we exclude through our prejudices, discrimination,
racism, sexism, ageism, homophobia, and so on. My mind would
race around in circles in this arena of exclusion. Then I caught
myself. Why am I doing this? There are plenty of books published on the different "isms" and how they exclude. What can
I say that has not been said? What is needed is a body of literature on the other side of the equation—how do we include?
With that I would attempt to focus on the subject of inclusion
again. After going through this pattern a few times, I finally
gave in to the need to dwell in the arena of exclusion. I figured
that if I wrote about exclusion for at least a short while, I
could exorcize and cleanse my mind of it so that I could spend
the rest of my energy on describing inclusion. This short play
and the pages that follow are the result of that endeavor.

1

A Dialogue between Two Children of God

Child 1:   God loves me.

Child 2:   God loves me too.

Child 1:   How can that be?

Child 2:   Why not?

Child 1:   Because God loves me.

Child 2:   That doesn't mean God can't love me.

Child 1:   Yes, it does.

Child 2:   Why?

Child 1:   Because I'm older and God loved me first.

Child 2:   That's not fair.

Child 1:   You don't expect God to love me all these years and then suddenly change his mind and love you just because you show up, do you?

Child 2:   Why can't God love more than one person?

Child 1:   Of course God can do that. It's just that God can't love you.

Child 2:   Why?

Child 1:   Because I don't like you.

Child 2:   What does that have to do with anything?

Child 1:   If God loves me and I don't like you, how can God possibly love you?

Child 2:   You're mean.

Child 1:   Say all you want, but you won't get God to love you.

Child 2:   Why?

Child 1:   Because I told him not to.

Child 2:   You can't tell God what to do!

Child 1:   Of course I can. God and I are real buddies.

Child 2: I don't think God likes being told what to do.

Child 1: You can if he loves you.

Child 2: I think you're going to hell.

Child 1: What?!

Child 2: God says, "Don't judge, lest you be judged."

Child 1: Where did you hear that?

Child 2: It's in the Bible. Since you judged me, I will tell God to judge you, so you are definitely going to hell.

Child 1: You can't do that.

Child 2: If you can tell God what to do, so can I.

Child 1: But you don't even know God.

Child 2: I don't know *your* god, but I know mine.

Child 1: Are you saying there are two different gods?

Child 2: Yeah, one loves you, and one loves me. And I don't think they get along in heaven.

Child 1: That's because my god is better.

Child 2: No, my god is nicer.

Child 1: My god is stronger

Child 2: My god is smarter.

Child 1: My god is bigger.

Child 2: My god is prettier.

Child 1: Wait a minute. This doesn't sound right.

Child 2: What doesn't sound right?

Child 1: I thought there is only one God.

Child 2: Where did you hear that?

Child 1: It says so in the Bible.

Child 2: Then your god must be a fake.

Child 1: No, my god is the real one, and your god must be Satan.

Child 2:   How dare you insult my god!

Child 1:   You are going to burn in the eternal fire of hell, Satan-worshiper!

Child 2:   You are going to be chopped up into a million pieces for insulting my god!

Child 1:   I hate you.

Child 2:   I hate you too.

Child 1:   I'll kill you.

Child 2:   I'll kill you first because the real god is on my side.

Child 1:   No, you have Satan on your side; you will definitely die first.

(They fight. Then one kills the other and goes on to argue with another child of God.)

Like the two children in this fictional play, we also have the tendency to exclude others just because they are different. Furthermore, for religious groups, we often bring God into the situation to justify our acts of exclusion. I wish I could say that all of us are born with an accepting attitude that appreciates differences, but in reality we tend to react to differences in negative and exclusive ways, especially early in our lives. For example, when young boys or girls discover the existence of the opposite sex, their reaction is not "Isn't that interesting? Let me learn more about you." Rather, their initial reaction is most likely a negative one, so they form boy groups and girl groups that are exclusive of each other. Over time, as we mature, we work through these initially negative reactions and learn to accept and appreciate the differences between genders. We even go out of our way to learn to live with the opposite sex, as demonstrated by the large quantity of literature addressing the differences between men and women published in the 1980s and 1990s.

However, the impulse to use exclusion as a means to deal with other kinds of differences remains with most of us even into adulthood. We have a yearning for stability and the familiar. By excluding those who are different, we don't have to work so hard to interact with new faces with "foreign" backgrounds and histories. In our comfortable group, we know all the rules; we know what to expect from each other; and we can be ourselves. But the world as God has created it is full of diversity. No matter how hard we try to isolate ourselves from these diversities, they are all around us. The moment we step outside our homes into our neighborhoods, our schools, or our workplaces, we cannot help but encounter people who are different. The differences that we have to deal with are, first of all, those basic diversity dimensions that exist within the human family—ethnicity, racial identity, gender, age, physical ability, and sexual orientation.

Beyond the above basic dimensions of diversity, which are mostly unchangeable, are other diversity dimensions we must consider, such as education, marital status, parental status, geographic location, work experience, military experience, religion, and economic status.[1] I would add theological difference as a dimension that most churches need to be aware of in considering the spectrum of diversity.

We may presume people who are different to be a threat to the safety and stability of our community. In order to protect ourselves from this perceived threat, we sometimes exclude others by insulating ourselves from them, or by shutting others out. We exclude others by ostracizing them, engaging in outright rejection of the differing others. We discriminate against them. We segregate them. We put up rules and criteria for acceptance, and then pronounce that there is no exception. We make up lies about how they are inferior and suggest that they might even be inhuman.

As I was writing the above paragraph, I realized the enormous number of words in the English language that we have

---

[1]The list of primary and secondary dimensions of diversity follow closely the diversity list provided by Marilyn Loden and Judy B. Rosener, *Workforce America! Managing Employee Diversity as a Vital Resource* (Homewood, Ill.: Business One Irwin, 1991).

available to describe exclusion: *omission, ostracism, segregation, apartheid, banishment, deletion, deportation, discrimination, elimination, exemption, exile, expulsion, exception, expurgation, rejection, removal,* and so on. When I think about verbs that we use to exclude, there are even more choices: *ban, bar, blackball, blacklist, boycott, cut off, delete, disregard, drop, eject, eliminate, excommunicate, expel, forbid, insulate, isolate, omit, ostracize, overlook, prevent, prohibit, reject, segregate, separate, shun, shut out,* and so on.

"What about words for inclusion in the English language?" I started to wonder. "What words are available to me in writing a book on the subject of inclusion?" So I looked in the thesaurus that was available in my computer's word processing software. I was shocked to find only three synonyms for inclusion: *insertion, addition,* and *enclosure.* On further examination, I noticed these three words were all meant to be used to describe the inclusion of objects, not people. I then checked for synonyms of the verb form of inclusion. I was happy to discover that there were more choices in the verb department, but again the choices were mostly verbs describing inclusion of objects — for example, *comprise, consist of, constitute, contain, entail, cover, insert, interject,* and so forth. When I eliminated those verbs that imply inclusion of objects only, I was left with *embody, embrace, encompass, incorporate,* and *involve.*

No wonder we are so ready to dive into the language and action of exclusion when we are faced with a group or person who is different. Our language, which is indicative of our cultural values, supplies a long list of expressions for exclusion but gives very little support for expressions of inclusion. And most expressions of inclusion are of objects, not of people. As a result, many of our efforts in the past to include people have treated those human beings that we were trying to include as objects to be moved around. Inclusion then became inserting the right number of people of each kind into the organization so that the organization would consist of the right percentage of the necessary different kinds of people. We paid little attention to what happened to them once they were "inserted."

Perhaps one of the reasons for the scarcity of words to articulate the inclusion of people is that the inclusion of people is a fairly new concept in the English language. Another reason may be that inclusion seems much more complicated than exclusion. Exclusion is simple. Once we reject the others, we don't have to deal with them anymore. We can go back to business as usual—no change, no hassle, no worries. It's clean. It requires little time, money, and energy. Inclusion involves a great deal of thinking and listening when we take into consideration others' experience, history, feelings, and so forth. Inclusion requires time and energy to follow up after a group or person has been physically included. It requires that everyone readjust. It requires change. Once a group is embraced in our circle, we have to live with its members for an unspecified period of time. That prospect can be very unsettling.

In all accounts, exclusion seems to be the more appealing choice when it comes to dealing with people who are different. This may be the reason I kept getting stuck in writing and thinking about exclusion when I was trying to articulate inclusion. This may be why we unconsciously choose exclusion time and again as a means to address differences.

Not only do we go straight to acts of exclusion ourselves, we also project our need to exclude onto God through our selective use of the Bible. We are quick to quote chapters and verses to support exclusion. After all, didn't Jesus drive the money changers out of the temple at Jerusalem? Didn't Jesus rail against the scribes and the Pharisees?(Mt. 23:1–36; Lk. 11:37–54) Didn't Jesus say that it was harder for a rich person to enter the kingdom of heaven than to put a camel through the eye of a needle? (Mt. 19:16 30; Mk. 10:17 31; Lk. 18:18–30) Didn't Jesus say that at the end the Son of man will separate the sheep and the goats and that the sheep will be welcome and the goats will be excluded? (Mt. 25:31 46) Didn't Paul excommunicate many people from the church? Didn't Paul say that women were to be submissive to men? We can exclude almost anybody who doesn't fit our ideas of what a good Christian is and blame it all on God, Jesus, Paul, and whomever else we can drum up to support exclusion.

There is no point in my arguing that Jesus or Paul or any of the major personalities in the Bible acted exclusively. They did, and so do everyone and every organization, especially the church. Jesus, in order to extend the salvation of God to the excluded—the unclean, the sinners, the tax collectors, the Gentiles, and so on—acted and spoke in judgmental, exclusive terms against the rich, the powerful, and the leaders of the established religion of his time. Jesus, in his passion to uphold the integrity and sacredness of God's ministry, challenged and drove out those who desecrated the temple of God.

Jesus' exclusive acts were directed at those who were already in the established religious organizations of his time, especially those who wielded power and influence in religious circles, people such as the scribes and the Pharisees and very often the rich. Jesus rejected their disregard for the essence of the Torah. Jesus rejected their using the law as an instrument of exclusion rather than as a framework for compassion and justice. Jesus rejected them because they should have known better and should have been prepared for the coming of the kingdom in which they would be judged by their acts of compassion and inclusion. They were to be accountable to God as the stewards of God's ministry, and they were charged with having to "keep awake therefore, for [they] know neither the day nor the hour" (Mt. 25:13).

In the early Christian church communities, acts of exclusion reflected concerns for the health of the formation of a fairly new community. Many of its community principles were derived from the Jewish community. The following passage, which was ascribed to Jesus by Matthew, parallels the Jewish community principles of the time.

> If another member of the church sins against you, go and point out the fault when the two of you are alone. If the member listens to you, you have regained that

one. But if you are not listened to, take one or two others along with you, so that every word may be confirmed by the evidence of two or three witnesses. If the member refuses to listen to them, tell it to the church; and if the offender refuses to listen even to the church, let such a one be to you as a Gentile and a tax collector.

Matthew 18:15–17

Notice the threefold process of interpersonal approaches in dealing with the member who sinned. Only when the interpersonal approaches failed was the person to be treated as a Gentile or a tax collector as the last resort. For the Jewish community of Jesus' time, to be treated as a Gentile or a tax collector was to be excommunicated. However, Jesus himself did not follow that rule of the community. He interacted with Gentiles and tax collectors and sinners by eating with them, being touched by them, and extending his healing power to them. If we are to imitate Jesus in our ministries, we have to balance our acts of exclusion with our acts of compassion and forgiveness. This might be a confusing contradiction, but it is what we are called to do if we take the whole of the gospel seriously. I want to explore this seeming contradiction further in the writings of Paul, to whom are attributed, in the life of the early church, various acts of excommunication.

Paul was concerned with the formation of the church when he had to make exclusive judgment. "For what have I to do with judging those outside? Is it not those who are inside that you are to judge? God will judge those outside. 'Drive out the wicked person from among you' " (1 Cor. 5:12–13). Paul was very clear that when it came to judgment that involved exclusion, it was only to be exercised among those within the community. Paul was saying to the members of the newly born church that they who knew Jesus as the Messiah should know better what was required of them and that they were accountable both to one another and to God. Judgment on those outside the community was a different story with a different set of criteria.

Paul, even though he was identified as the one who ex-communicated, actually takes a soft approach to maintaining and protecting the early church community. In 2 Thessalonians 3:10, he prescribed withholding food from someone who was unwilling to work.

And for the offense of disobedience, he prescribed, "Have nothing to do with them, so that they may be ashamed" (2 Thess. 3:14). But he added, in his softer voice, tempered no doubt by his obedience to Jesus' ministry of compassion, "Do not regard them as enemies, but warn them as believers" (2 Thess. 3:15). Paul's compassionate side showed even more in the following passage, in which he was trying to soften the punishment he had prescribed earlier for a particular member of the community in Corinth.

> But if anyone has caused pain, he has caused it not to me, but to some extent—not to exaggerate it—to all of you. This punishment by the majority is enough for such a person; so now instead you should forgive and console him, so that he may not be overwhelmed by excessive sorrow. So I urge you to reaffirm your love for him…Anyone whom you forgive, I also forgive. What I have forgiven, if I have forgiven anything, has been for your sake in the presence of Christ.
>
> *2 Corinthians 2:5–10*

In both the letters to the Thessalonians and Corinthians, the early church did not seem to have very rigid rules regarding excommunication. The rules were based on Jewish community law and, in the last case cited, were modified in accordance with the circumstances. Paul's actions of judgment were always balanced by his yearning for the community, the body of Christ, to be inclusive, compassionate, and forgiving. But most of all, Paul yearned for unity within the community of Christ.

But avoid stupid controversies, genealogies, dissensions,
and quarrels about the law, for they are unprofitable
and worthless. After a first and second admonition, have
nothing more to do with anyone who causes divisions,
since you know that such a person is perverted and
sinful, being self-condemned.

Titus 3:9–10

Paul's passion for holding the community together forced
him to reject anyone who caused division. Jesus was concerned
with compassion and the inclusion of the weak, the outcasts,
and the outsiders. Therefore, anyone who did not exercise compassion was rejected. In both cases, they were speaking to those
who were inside—Jesus speaking to the insiders of the Jewish
religious community, and Paul speaking to the insiders of the
early Christian community. Again, I do not dispute the fact
that both Jesus and Paul acted exclusively. But I am quick to
point out that the acts of exclusion were a last resort in most
of the cases. I also want to point out that the stories, acts, and
quotes from the Bible that support inclusion far outnumber
those dealing with exclusion. Many of the incidents and stories of inclusion concerned the inclusion of those who were
outsiders.

I can readily think of story after story, quote after quote
that support inclusion from the Christian scriptures—the parable of the prodigal son (Lk. 15:11–32); the parable of the lost
sheep (Mt. 18:10–14; Lk. 15:1–7); the parable of the good Samaritan (Lk. 10:29–37); Jesus' healing of lepers (Lk. 5:12–16;
17:11–19; Mt. 8:1–3; Mk. 1:40–45); Jesus' talking to the Samaritan woman at the well (Jn. 4:1–42); Jesus' discourse with
the Canaanite woman who asked Jesus to heal her child (Mt.
15:21–28; Mk. 7:24–30); Jesus' dealing with the woman who
was caught in adultery (Jn. 7:53—8:11) and with the woman
with a reputation, weeping and wiping his feet with her hair
(Lk. 7:36–50); Jesus' healing of the woman with the hemorrhage

(Lk. 8:42–48); the healing of the centurion's slave (Lk. 7:1–10); Jesus' healing of the son of the Gentile military officer (Jn. 4:46–54); and Jesus' commissioning the disciples to be his witnesses in Jerusalem, in all Judea and Samaria, and to the ends of the earth (Acts 1:8).

Many of the passages cited above record Jesus' dissatisfaction with the established religion of the time's use of the laws as a vehicle to exclude the powerless, poor, and weak. He was also dissatisfied with the exclusion of the Gentiles and Samaritans from the salvation of God, which was to be for all people and nations. It was so easy for the religious leaders to deal with differences by using exclusion. They only needed to apply the laws and it was done. According to the rules, if you were a Samaritan, you were not one of us, and, therefore, we would not even talk to you. But Jesus not only talked to Samaritans, he extended the salvation of God to them. According to the rules, if you were a sinner, you were therefore excluded. Jesus ate with sinners and tax collectors, prostitutes and beggars. According to the rules, children and women had no voice in the community. Jesus included children and women in many of his acts and sayings and parables. Jesus spent much of his ministry countering and resisting exclusion and acted in such a radical, inclusive way that the establishment had to stop him. Jesus' ministry has forever changed the boundary of his religious community—from one of fast and easy exclusion of those considered different to one of inclusion based on compassion and justice.

Paul also recognized this ministry of inclusion. One must remember that Paul was a Pharisee, one of those who at that time followed and applied the letter of the law. His conversion in recognizing Jesus as the Messiah changed his perception of the law forever. In his energetic and passionate letter to the Galatians, he articulated this change very clearly.

> Now before faith came, we were imprisoned and guarded under the law until faith would be revealed. Therefore the law was our disciplinarian until Christ

came, so that we might be justified by faith. But now that faith has come, we are no longer subject to a disciplinarian, for in Christ Jesus you are all children of God through faith. As many of you as were baptized into Christ have clothed yourselves with Christ.

Galatians 3:23–27

Now that faith has come, the process of deciding who is in and who is out of the community of God has changed from a rule-based, right-or-wrong, exclusive approach to one that is Christ-centered. Look at the acts of inclusion that follow in the community of Christ recorded in the Christian scriptures: the Pentecost event, where "Jews from every nation" gathered and heard "God's deeds of power" (Acts 2:1–47); the commissioning of the seven Hellenists to solve the dispute about exclusion by the Hebrews (Acts 6:1–7); the conversion of Cornelius, the first Gentile convert by Peter (Acts 10:1–48); Paul and Barnabas' visit to Jerusalem in defense of the Gentile Christians (Acts 15:1–35); Paul's image of the body of Christ as inclusive of people with different gifts(1 Cor. 12:12–31); Paul's words on not passing premature judgment (1 Cor. 4:1–5); and Paul's words following the above Galatians passage:

There is no longer Jew or Greek, there is no longer slave or free, there is no longer male and female; for all of you are one in Christ Jesus.

Galatians 3:28

In conclusion, the language of exclusion in the Bible was addressed to those who were already part of the religious community. Even in these cases, exclusion was the last resort. One of the major criteria for exclusion was whether one acted compassionately and inclusively toward the outcasts. Jesus and Paul used totally different sets of language and actions when addressing those who were outside the community. When we use the language of exclusion that was meant for insiders to block outsiders who are trying to get in, we are misusing the scripture. Sayings, acts, and images of inclusion stemming from Christ's ministry recorded in the Christian scriptures far out-number those of exclusion. Exclusion has its place in the preservation of the community, but it should not overshadow the work of including those who are outside the community. Inclusion of outsiders weighs much more than the preservation of the existing community.

My plea to readers is that you resist the impulse to exclude. I invite you to reject the temptation to blame God and the Bible for your acts of exclusion. My hope is that the pages that follow will clarify and define the inclusion process from a Christian perspective. I pray that this book will encourage you to begin addressing any differences you may have with the inclusion process. Even when you have strong urges to walk the easy path of exclusion, I invite you to take the advice of Robert Frost's poem (and the title of Scott Peck's book), to take "the road less traveled." Choose the road of inclusion—a more difficult road that involves much more time, energy, patience, and faith in God through Christ, who will lead, push, redirect, and nurture you along the way.

2

This Fellow Welcomes Sinners and Eats with Them

Sitting in an exploratory meeting with a church committee, I stared at the mission statement posted prominently on the wall. It read "St. Mary's is a loving, diverse, inclusive community of people who…" After some discussion regarding the purpose of our meeting, one of the committee members said in frustration, "We are still an over-fifty, white congregation with no sign of growth after living with this mission statement for five years. We must be doing something wrong." The request for my presence was to teach them how to be more inclusive.

This congregation, like so many organizations, misconstrues describing itself as inclusive as becoming inclusive. First, it is problematic to use the word *inclusive* as an adjective to describe a static entity. We use the term *inclusive community* as if it were a measurable, quantitative state of the organization that one can achieve. With that misconception, many of our approaches to inclusion, such as affirmative action and quotas, only focus on the visible outcome. We "include" people in the same way a group of kids divides up different colored M&Ms by making sure each kid has the same quantity of each color.

An inclusive community or organization cannot be a static entity. Every defined organization is by nature exclusive. When an organization declares its existence, it defines its boundary and, therefore, defines who is part of the organization and who is not. These organization boundaries can be explicit, as in a mission statement, but they can also be implicit, as in a circle of friends. These boundaries are essential to the maintenance, identity, and sometimes survival of the organization.

We all belong to a number of exclusive organizations and communities—our family, our circle of friends, our work organizations, our college alumni/alumnae organization, our health club, and so on. The question is not whether these organizations or communities to which we belong are exclusive because they are exclusive by nature. As we further explore the concept of an inclusive community, the questions we need to ask are: How does a community act or react when its explicit and implicit boundaries are being challenged? Does it act exclusively or inclusively?

The challenge of a community's boundaries can come in various forms.

1. The most obvious one occurs when a previously excluded group or person wants to be part of the community. How does a community react to that? Do we say, "Because you don't look like us, you are out?" Or do we say, "Let us think about this. Let us talk more about this," which might be the beginning of a more inclusive process.

2. Another kind of boundary challenge appears in churches that have experienced major shifts in demographics. Many are saying, "We know there are people of different cultures, lifestyles, or ages in our neighborhood. We tried to welcome them, but they would not come, and when they came, they would not stay. What do we do now?" This boundary challenge comes from within the community when it yearns to welcome another but is unable to do so.

3. A third kind of boundary challenge comes in the form of complaints from people who are already part of the community but feel that they are excluded in decision making, in leadership, and/or in participating fully in the life of the community. This kind of boundary challenge also comes from within, but the challenge is targeted at the implicit boundary within the explicit boundary of the community. That is, even though the community explicitly says that it has already included the persons or groups in question, those persons do not feel as if all avenues of opportunity are open to them within the community. Because of this, some "members" have come up against implicit boundaries that exclude them from being fully part of the community. If this kind of implicit boundary challenge is not addressed constructively, the group that has less influence and power in the community—the implicitly excluded group—will leave.

4. An example of another kind of boundary challenge is the recent need for congregations to explore working together in order to survive their shrinking resources and the rising cost of maintenance of their buildings and paid staff. This kind of exploration may include amalgamation of congregations or clusters of congregations sharing leadership and program resources. On a bigger scale, in recent years there have been discussions on amalgamation of conferences, presbyteries, and even denominations. In these negotiations, the boundaries of all the communities involved are being challenged.

In order to examine how a community acts when its boundary is being challenged, we must first look at the concept of "boundary function." (I don't like jargon, but I am trying to find a quick way to refer to the process by which a person or group becomes a member of a community.) What is the community's leadership and organizational structure that enables or disables a person from becoming a full member?

The boundary function of a community is the mechanism by which a person or group is accepted as a full member of the community—is transformed from being "them" to "us."

A community is like a body, which has its normal functions of absorbing substances that are beneficial and rejecting or excreting substances that are harmful. For example, our kidneys, liver, and intestines function in this discriminating fashion to keep our bodies healthy. If these organs malfunction, the body retains too many harmful substances and eventually poisons itself. Most human organizations function in a similar way by welcoming those who would enhance the organization and rejecting those who would be harmful to the life of the organization. This boundary function enables a community to define itself and to maintain its existing boundaries so that the community can continue to function and accomplish its stated purpose.

Sometimes the boundary function of a community may be too loose, resulting in the community's accepting everyone without reservation. When a community does not expel those who would be harmful to the community, it poisons itself; the community's life becomes diminished, and it may die. At the other extreme, the boundary function of a community may be so tight that it rejects everyone who is not exactly like those already in the community. This kind of unhealthy boundary function is like an anorexic person who stops eating and starves to death.

Most organizations in the world use a very simple boundary function to maintain and protect their identity and boundaries. (See diagram 2.1.) Most organizations consider the space within their boundaries as a safe zone in which, as the label connotes, the members feel safe and secure. In this environment, we are with people who are like us. We do not have to work hard to get along with them. We prefer not to change. Only those who do not present a threat to the organization can enter.

Diagram 2.1: Exclusive Boundary Function

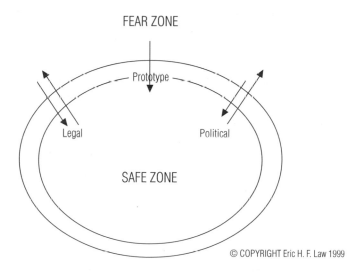

FEAR ZONE

— Prototype —

Legal   Political

SAFE ZONE

© COPYRIGHT Eric H. F. Law 1999

For an organization that tends to act exclusively, immediately beyond its safe zone lies the fear zone. The fear zone is the world "out there" that presents threats to our safety and stability as an organization. This is the place where we do not want to set foot because if we do, we may become so afraid that we will cease to function; we will shut down, and we might lash out and fight in order to return to our safe zone. An exclusive organization has very little or no room between the safe zone and the fear zone. Its members are easily threatened if they are being pushed or pulled out of their safe zone. Any pushing from the inside will move people very quickly into the fear zone. Any pulling or stretching from the outside will be resisted. This narrow space between the safe zone and the fear zone provides little room or time to negotiate, explore, or engage in dialogue. It has no room for grace.

The boundary function of such an exclusive organization is controlled by three basic mechanisms:

1. ***Comparison with a prototype.*** An exclusive organization
has a standard, a prototype, or a set of required elements
against which it measures newcomers to determine
whether they are "qualified" to be part of the
organization. If you fit that standard and look the part,
you are in. If you don't, you are out. As in a private club,
if you have the right education, you are in. If you have
the right income level, you are in. If you wear the right
shoes, you are in. If you have the right skin color, you
are in. Most organizations use this simple form of boundary function to define themselves based on skills, age,
knowledge, size, gender, ethnicity, nationality, economic
status, language, and so forth. For most organizations,
this type of exclusive boundary function is commonly
accepted. For example, a job interview is a major component of an organization's boundary function. The job
description sets the standard or prototype description
of the kind of employee for whom the organization is
looking. Those who do not fit that description will have
very little chance of being hired. A football team would
most likely reject those who are small. A basketball team
would most likely reject those who are short. A casting
director of a musical would most likely reject those who
cannot sing.

2. ***The legal operation.*** Even when you fit the prototype
and enter the organization, you still have to follow the
explicit and implicit rules of the organization. If you do
not, you will most likely be expelled. For example, after
you are hired for a job, if you do not follow the office
protocols, you may be let go at the end of the probation
period. If you are big, tall, and strong like a football player
but do not follow the rules of the game, you are not
allowed to play. If you have a dancer's body but in the
rehearsal of the show do not follow the choreographer's
direction, you will not make it to the opening.

Sometimes a person may not fit the prototype 100 percent but is allowed to join the organization because he or she follows all the rules. Very often, such a person is watched all the time and must be extra careful and dutiful in following the rules in order to stay in the organization.

3. **The political operation.** Even when you fit the prototype and follow all the rules, you may still be excluded if you do not get along with the influential and powerful members of the organization. They are the gatekeepers of the organization; everyone who enters the organization must meet with their approval. For example, if you have all the qualifications to do a job and know and follow all the protocols but do not get along with your boss, you may not survive long on the job. Sometimes a person may not have all the qualifications but will be allowed to join the organization only because he or she knows the influential people. For example, an actress may not sing or act well but is cast as the star of a musical because she knows the producer. Sometimes different groups within the organization may gain or lose power and influence through political maneuvers. In democratic organizations, the political process is handled by campaigning and voting. In some organizations, the political process may involve hostile takeover—those who have the most money or military force take control of the boundary of the organization.

This exclusive boundary function is very appealing because it is the most simple way to deal with differences. It requires very little time. All a community needs to do is to compare a person or group against the prototype, the standard, or investigate whether that person or group follows all the required rules. That process should determine whether the person or group is included or not. If the newcomers are in, they have the common qualities that existing members have and should get along fine with everyone. If they are out, the community does not have to deal with them anymore. It is simple. It is clean. It is quick. It is effortless. Many communities have a tendency to go straight to this simple, exclusive way of dealing with differences. In church communities, we often use this simple boundary function unconsciously.

"Help us attract more youth" is one of the most popular requests from churches seeking assistance. In most cases, as we discuss the concerns about the declining number of youth, some church members will complain, "The youth today don't appreciate the traditions of the church." Or they grumble, "Their music is not music at all." Their request for attracting youth mutates into two forms:

1. What can we do to the youth to make them more like us?

2. How can we do what we do better so that they will come?

Their boundary function requires potential youth members to change, to adapt to the way of life of those already in the community. The prototype of a "good" member is the adult already in the community. If youth are to be part of the community, they have to follow the rules. For example, a church may not play music that youth like in worship because the adults continue to hold the power in the community. Their implicit purpose is to protect and preserve the traditions of the community. Here a church community speaks of inclusion, but remains caught in the exclusive ways of the world.

Sometimes even the communities that actively try to be inclusive can fall into using this exclusive boundary function without being aware of it. When I was in college in the mid-'70s, the campus ministry of which I was a part introduced me to the concept of inclusive language. At that time, I had been in the United States for four years and was still learning the

English language. The concept of inclusive language was odd because in the Chinese language, male and female pronouns sound the same, and God is referred to with a special pronoun, written differently but pronounced identically as the pronouns for *he* and *she*. Nevertheless, I understood that the way we then used the English language consistently excluded women. Furthermore, referring to God as "he" exclusively could create the perception that women are not of the holy and therefore inferior. I supported this endeavor to promote inclusive language wholeheartedly and was willing to adapt to this new way of using the English language.

By the time I attended seminary five years later, inclusive language had fossilized into a set of rules to be enforced. Anyone who did not use the proper inclusive language in the classroom, in the hallway, and in the courtyard was immediately looked upon as a sexist person, especially when noninclusive language was used by a man. We became language police, watching every "he or she" being used cumbersomely in our everyday conversation. God is neither he nor she; God is just God without any images that imply a gender reference. The seminary community no doubt had struggled with the language issues for many years, and the intention to include women in the way we use language was good and should be supported. But when this movement, which started out as a means of inclusion, became an instrument of exclusion, something had gone wrong. Instead of explaining to those who did not use the "proper inclusive language" that what they said had an exclusive effect on women in the community, we simply ostracized them by telling them they were wrong. We seemed to have lost the original intent of the movement— to include. The "rules" of inclusive language became a simple, exclusive boundary function for many liberal communities. We simply applied the rules to determine who was in and who was out, even when this set of rules was for the purpose of inclusion. Fortunately, by the mid-'80s, when I was graduating from seminary, the inclusive language movement had moved beyond being a set of rules and instead became one of balanced usage of diverse images in referring to God.

The exclusive boundary function is useful for most organizations in the world, but it is not adequate for use in the Christian community. In the Christian community, we cannot have hard-and-fast rules to determine who is in or out. The Christian community claims to be the body of Christ. In the body of Christ, diversity is a given in which many different gifts are welcome. The Christian community takes the body analogy comprehensively. Just like the body, which must accept a diversity of food to maintain its chemical balance and therefore its health, the body of Christ must include a diversity of people to do Christ's ministry in the world. If we only eat one kind of food, our system will eventually break down. If a Christian community accepts only one type of person, it will not be able to respond creatively to the changes in the world around it. "If you love those who love you, what credit is that to you? For even sinners love those who love them" (Lk. 6:32).

Jesus spent much of his earthly ministry resisting the exclusive boundary function as personified by the gospels' portrayal of the scribes and Pharisees.

> Now when the Pharisee who had invited him saw it, he said to himself, "If this man were a prophet, he would have known who and what kind of woman this is who is touching him—that she is a sinner."
>
> *Luke 7:39*

> And the Pharisees and the scribes were grumbling and saying, "This fellow welcomes sinners and eats with them."
>
> *Luke 15:2*

They were grumbling about Jesus' not following the law and not respecting those who had power and influence in the religious establishment. In their legalistic mind-set, one had to follow the law or at least appear to do so. Only then could one be accepted into the religious community and the social fabric of the society. Their idea of a good person—the prototype—was, of course, their self-righteous selves. When Jesus welcomed those who were considered sinners to eat with him and to touch him, he rejected the legalistic and power-based boundary function of the Pharisees and the scribes in favor of something more personal and compassionate, but confusing. The boundary function that Jesus used seemed to require more time, energy, and reflection than a simple comparison of the outsiders and the prototype. It seemed to have a complicated standard that was not as black and white as a set of rules that one was supposed to follow. It was not clear who had the power to determine who was in or out. It seemed to be inconsistent and ambiguous. How did a community with such a fuzzy boundary function establish its boundary at all? How did such a community maintain its identity if it constantly welcomed strangers who were not like those already in the community?

This uncertainty regarding its boundary has been a continuous struggle for the Christian church since its beginning. A very early example recorded in Acts was the struggle over the Antioch Christians' questioning whether they needed to practice all the Jewish laws before becoming believers. Christians throughout history have struggled with the question of who is in and who is out. The heresy trials and the division of the church—first with the Orthodox and then the Protestants—were all issues of boundary definitions. In the twentieth century, the question of excommunication, women's roles in the church, and the debate over the gay and lesbian issue are all part of the struggle to define our institutional church boundaries and are challenges to the church's existing boundary function.

One of the purposes of boundaries is to protect the institution so that it will survive. With this assumption, the church responded to the challenges to its boundary in the same way as most secular institutions. On one level, this is to be expected because the church, along with being the body of Christ, is, after all, a human organization. On a deeper level, as shown to us by Christ, the Christian community is challenged to look at the purpose of drawing a boundary differently. Boundaries are not only there to reject those who are considered harmful to the community; they are also there to uphold the identity and vitality of the community, making sure that the community succeeds in accomplishing its purpose. One of the central missions of the Christian community is to welcome those who are excluded. This inclusive stand is at the heart of the complicated boundary function of the Christian community. In other words, the boundary function of a faithful Christian community begins with inclusion.

Yet in order to survive, the church has to maintain its identity by defining its boundary and protecting it. The Christian boundary function must take into consideration the tension between wanting to be widely inclusive and being able to survive as an institution that will carry on its mission. Each time the Christian community extends its boundary to take into consideration another group's experience and context, it upsets the equilibrium of the community. Each time, the Christian community has to struggle to find its way back to a somewhat stable state again. But often before it can do that, it is faced with another challenge to its boundary by another new group of strangers—outsiders to whom the Christian community is called to extend itself again. By rejecting the simple, exclusive boundary function of the religious establishment of his time, Jesus pushed his followers and the church out of their safe zone into an area that required constant reflection and reconnection with God as a living, compassionate being. Therefore, from its beginning, the Christian boundary function is very complicated, multilayered, time-consuming, and sometimes contradictory. It can create great uncertainty and confusion. It definitely requires risk taking.

In order to understand and live this often unsettling Christian inclusive boundary function, we must first understand grace. Only by the grace of God can we have the openness required to extend ourselves to listen and understand another's points of view with which we might disagree. Only by the grace of God can we have the patience to work through our differences. The abundant grace of God as shown to us by Jesus Christ will keep us secure in the midst of seeming chaos. In the grace of God, we can let go of our insecurity, let go of our rigid rules, let go of our power, and invite Christ to help us discern the will of our gracious God in the ministry of inclusion.

3

Crumbs, Leftovers, and Grace

Jesus left that place and went away to the district of
Tyre and Sidon. Just then a Canaanite woman from
that region came out and started shouting, "Have mercy
on me, Lord, Son of David; my daughter is tormented
by a demon." But he did not answer her at all. And his
disciples came and urged him, saying, "Send her away,
for she keeps shouting after us." He answered, "I was
sent only to the lost sheep of the house of Israel." But
she came and knelt before him, saying, "Lord, help me."
He answered, "It is not fair to take the children's food
and throw it to the dogs." She said, "Yes, Lord, yet even
the dogs eat the crumbs that fall from their masters'
table." Then Jesus answered her, "Woman, great is your
faith! Let it be done for you as you wish." And her
daughter was healed instantly.

Matthew 15:21–28 (Mark 7:24–30)

The reaction from Jesus and the disciples was at first indif-
ference and then rejection. "Send her away," they said, "for she
keeps shouting after us." They too chose to deal with this challenge of their boundaries with the simple exclusive boundary

29

function. Since this woman was not a Jew, she was not included in salvation history. In a very uncharacteristic style, Jesus
even said it out loud, "It is not fair to take the children's food
and throw it to the dogs." Yet she persisted. After a somewhat
witty discourse between the woman and Jesus about "crumbs,"
Jesus included her by healing her daughter and commended
her for her faith.

One can imagine a storyteller in an early Jewish Christian
community telling this story as a rebuttal to those who believe
in a very narrow definition of a believer of Christ—that a
believer had to follow the Jewish laws first before being accepted fully in the community. One can also imagine a storyteller in an early Gentile Christian community telling this story
with passion, suspense, and delight in Jesus' changing his mind
about the extent of God's salvation. We, who were considered
outsiders, not only could get in but could also change things,
even the mind of the Divine. Jesus commended this woman's
faith that dared to challenge the existing established rules, which
limited the sharing of the abundance of God's healing power.
Her faith knew firmly that there was not only enough grace
and blessing from God for the people of the Jewish community, but that the leftover crumbs were enough to feed every
tribe, race, and people on earth.

This was a story about negotiating and stretching boundaries. This was a story of moving from exclusion to inclusion.
This was a story about the abundant grace of God.

In the gospels of Matthew and Mark, before and after this
story are two more stories concerning food, leftovers and
grace—the feeding of the five thousand and the feeding of the
four thousand. I will concentrate on the first of these stories
for the purpose of our continuing exploration of the wonderful grace of God.

> When it was evening, the disciples came to him and
> said, "This is a deserted place, and the hour is now late;
> send the crowds away so that they may go into the
> villages and buy food for themselves." Jesus said to them,

"They need not go away; you give them something to eat." They replied, "We have nothing here but five loaves and two fish." And he said, "Bring them here to me." Then he ordered the crowds to sit down on the grass. Taking the fives loaves and the two fish, he looked up to heaven, and blessed and broke the loaves, and gave them to the disciples, and the disciples gave them to the crowds. And all ate and were filled; and they took up what was left over of the broken pieces, twelve baskets full. And those who ate were about five thousand men, besides women and children.

Matthew 14:15–21

The story of the feeding of the five thousand actually appears in all four gospels (Mk. 6:30–44; Lk. 9:10–17; and Jn. 6:1–14) with slight variations. The basic facts that appear in each of the four versions are these: Jesus blessed and broke the loaves, which fed more than five thousand people, and there were twelve baskets of leftovers. This congruency in the narratives affirms the immense significance of this story to the faith and life of the Christian church.

How could that be? we would ask with our practical minds. Twelve baskets of leftovers were definitely more than the five loaves of bread and two fish with which they started. Perhaps that is why we call this a miracle. The reason we cannot comprehend this event as anything but a miracle is because of the way we think about our resources. We tend to think of our resources as limited. Once they are gone, there will be no more! Society keeps telling us that there is not enough for everyone. This attitude can cause us to feel insecure. In the light of that insecurity, we may make keeping what we have and accumulating material things our main purpose in life. We may believe that the more we have, the more secure we can be. We may even go as far as to deprive others of their share of resources, surmising that if fewer people were sharing the limited resources, we would be sure to secure our share and possibly even more.

The disciples were thinking that way too. When Jesus said to them, "They need not go away; you give them something to eat," they looked at the limit of their five loaves and two fish and thought, *How could we possibly feed that many people? We hardly have enough for ourselves.* But Jesus was trying to teach them a different way of looking at our God-given resources. Jesus was trying to demonstrate to them a new way of knowing God's grace.

Let me share an experience in my childhood that might shed light on discerning what Jesus was trying teach us through this event. When I was young, my family always had guests for dinner. On any given day, there might be twelve to fifteen people at the dinner table. Dinner was a time of joyful sharing of food and stories. I thought we were quite wealthy, feeding so many people every night. Only when I was older, while talking to my mother about the good old days, did I find out that we were not rich at all. My mother told me that some days she only had three Hong Kong dollars to feed fifteen people. How could that be? I could not remember a day when there was not enough food! What my mother did with three dollars was a miracle in itself. If you asked her how she did it, she would tell you how she determined what to buy in what season and, more importantly, her techniques in bargaining. But I think there is more to this miracle than just knowing what to buy and how to bargain. Not only was everyone around the table filled every night, there were often leftovers. I believe the way we dealt with the leftovers at the dinner table is indicative of how this miracle was accomplished.

Toward the end of dinner, there was always something left on a plate in the middle of the table. Everyone would be staring at it, especially when it was a piece of meat, which was an occasional, special treat. But no one would make a move to take it. Then someone would say, "Why don't you take it, Grandma? You are the oldest." But my grandma would say, "No, I've been eating this stuff all my life. Give it to the little one. He's the youngest and needs the nourishment to grow up to be big and strong." I, being the youngest, and who also learned this ritual, would say, "No, not me. I am completely full because I have the smallest stomach. Give it to my oldest brother. He has an examination at school tomorrow. He needs it so he can do well." My oldest brother would say, "No, not me. Give it to my sister. She has a piano lesson tomorrow…" This ritual would go on around the table; each person would find an excuse not to take the leftover piece of food. While we offered it to each other, we also affirmed each other's worthiness in the family. As a result, the piece of meat would sit in the middle of the table, destined to be left over. It became a symbol of our appreciation of each other's worth. This leftover piece of food became a sign of the abundance we shared.

At the dinner table of my childhood, I learned a very important concept about our resources. This concept was very different from that which our society taught me. Society tells us that we should have more than others because of the belief that our resources are limited. At my childhood dinner table, I learned that there was an abundance of resources and that there was always enough. Moreover, there was always food left over. With this mind-set, it was a virtue to have less than another. In that security, we could give until we had less. This did not mean we would have nothing. It simply meant that we would have less, but enough. We were still going to be filled.

I think this may be what Jesus was trying to teach the disciples. One can imagine, as the disciples were handing the blessed and broken loaves to someone in the crowd, that person might have said, "No, I don't need this. I am not that hungry. Give it to someone who needs it more than I do." Another might have said, "I brought a little bit of my own food. I don't need it. Here, take some of mine. I won't be needing all of it. Give it to this person next to me." With that, she might have contributed to the food supply in the baskets while they were being passed around. If everyone acted with the understanding that there is always an abundance of resources and that, therefore, it is good to have less than someone else, there would always be leftovers. That might be the reason that the collected leftovers were more than the food they started with.

In the feeding of the five thousand, Jesus challenges us not to think of our God-given resources as limited. Instead, he wants us to know that God has given us an earth that can produce an abundance of resources. In that abundance, there is always enough for everyone. As Paul said to the Corinthians: "And God is able to provide you with every blessing in abundance, so that by always having enough of everything, you may share abundantly in every good work" (2 Cor. 9:8).

In our human insecurity, however, we ignore what Jesus taught us and insist that our resources are limited. In our fear of scarcity, we hold back and deprive others of this abundance. For example, if we added up all food production from the farming industry in North America, we could probably feed everyone in the world. No one would be hungry. And yet there are children who go to bed hungry every night. Each day people die of hunger. Something is very wrong. Jesus is trying to turn us around. We must repent and change our thinking regarding our resources—from an attitude of scarcity to one of abundance.

Not only do we apply this attitude of scarcity to food and material goods, we may also apply it to our spiritual life. We may think that God's blessing and grace is limited. We may think Christ's compassion is not enough to go around. Once it is gone, there will be none left. So the purpose of our spiritual life becomes doing things that will earn God's favor, as if God's grace is only given to those who are "good." Like the Pharisees and scribes as described in the Christian scriptures, we may follow the law to its letter and insist that others do the same. Like the Pharisees and the scribes, we may start judging others. "You are a sinner; therefore, you are not in God's favor and you do not deserve God's love." In denying others their share of God's grace, we may think that we are secure in our share and might get even more.

A community cannot act inclusively out of the assumption that God's grace is limited and scarce. In the fear of not being loved by God, we spend a lot of our energy and time enforcing the rules that we set for ourselves by thinking that they are God's rules. We use our political influence to protect our boundaries instead of letting God be the powerful one to shape our community. We narrow the margin between our fear zone and our safe zone and leave little room to extend our boundary to include another who might not look or act like us. There is no room for grace.

Only when a community operates on the assumption that there is always an abundance of God's grace can it be secure enough to open its boundaries to include another. An inclusive community must believe that Christ's compassion is boundless and God's love is so abundant that God can love everyone on earth—not just those of us who think we are doing what is right in God's sight, not just those who think and act like us. God's grace is extended to those with whom we do not get along, to those who we think are our enemies, to those who we think are sinners. That is why Christ came—to show us that God's grace is boundless. Jesus, who lived in the security of God's abundant grace, gave himself for us so that we could have life abundantly. Out of our gratefulness for God's graciousness, we respond with our good work, sharing God's grace with more and more people. When we realize that God's grace is so rich and full and abundant that there is enough for me and you and everyone and that there will always be leftovers, we will have the courage to imitate Christ, to give ourselves for others—to act inclusively.

But God, who is rich in mercy, out of the great love with which he loved us even when we were dead through our trespasses, made us alive together with Christ—by grace you have been saved—and raised us up with him and seated us with him in the heavenly places in Christ Jesus, so that in the ages to come he might show the immeasurable riches of his grace in kindness toward us in Christ Jesus. For by grace you have been saved through faith, and this is not our own doing; it is the gift of God—not the result of works, so that no one may boast.

Ephesians 2:4–9

Paul understood this abundant grace of God in a very personal way. God's grace was granted to him even when he was a Pharisee who persecuted Christians. It is out of this overwhelming experience of grace that he became an apostle, taking the gospel far beyond the Jewish community into the Gentile world and, for that matter, to the entire world. The above passage from Ephesians captures his understanding of the essence of God's grace.

According to Paul, grace is a gift. It is abundant and immeasurable. It is not something that we have earned by our "good work" or by our diligent obedience to the law. It is out of God's richness in mercy, kindness, and great love that this grace was given to us in spite of our sin. Furthermore, out of the generosity of God's grace, we are saved. Grace is manifested through Christ during his earthly ministry in the past, the present, and the future. We respond to grace with our faith—our belief in our being forgiven by the grace of God. In our thankfulness, we respond by doing good work imitating Christ—being the expression and the example of God's grace—in our words and action. In that way, grace multiplies through us (2 Cor. 4:15) and becomes contagious: "So that your words may give grace to those who hear" (Eph. 4:29).

The Christian inclusion process must be built on the foundation of this abundant grace of God. We respond to this amazing grace by leaving behind our preoccupation with scarcity and self-preservation and moving courageously toward extending our boundary, sharing this grace with strangers. In this grace, we recognize that each person is forgiven, blessed, and a child of God who has the right and privilege to share the abundance of God's creation, and we can trust God to provide for everyone whom we welcome into our circle. In this grace, we have the courage to deal with difficult issues created by our differences. We can be angry yet not sin; we can listen to difficult words of truth and not retreat; and we can negotiate with each other and even with God in truth, compassion, and faithfulness.

In a world where most organizations and institutions have little room for grace, where people who are different are dealt with through legalistic proceeding, political maneuver, and even violent destruction, the church community, as the body of Christ, must stretch its arms of compassion and justice to make room for grace.

Steadfast love and faithfulness will meet;

righteousness and peace will kiss each other.

Faithfulness will spring up from the ground,

and righteousness will look down from the sky.

Psalm 85:10–11

4

Making Room for Grace

I am the gate. Whoever enters by me will be saved, and will come in and go out and find pasture. The thief comes only to steal and kill and destroy. I came that they may have life, and have it abundantly.

John 10:9–10

I have heard this passage used by many Christians to support their exclusion of others. Their assumption is that if a person does not believe in the specific way that they do, that person is blocked from entering God's kingdom by Christ, who is the gate. The image of Christ that they use is that of a doorman, checking each person who is attempting to come in, and only those who fit the prototype—themselves—and follow the rules are allowed to enter. This interpretation of Christ as the gate is based on the assumption of limited grace—there is not enough grace to go around, so only those who are good enough will receive it.

On the contrary, Jesus was describing a much more dynamic process, using the symbol of the gate—"come in and go out and find pasture." This dynamic process is based on the spirituality of abundance—"I came that they may have life,

39

and have it abundantly." The way Jesus used the gate image connoted Christ as a gracious host, welcoming strangers to come in and share the abundance of love, joy, and life and sending guests out into the world to share the same. If Christ is the gate, then Christ is the boundary function of the Christian community. Therefore, we must first examine Jesus' action to understand how the Christian inclusion process works. We need to pay particular attention to how he dealt with people's exclusive attitudes.

In Luke 7:36–49, Jesus was invited to eat with the Pharisees. "A woman in the city, who was a sinner," stood behind Jesus, weeping, and bathed his feet with her tears and dried them with her hair. The Pharisees thought, "If this man were a prophet, he would have known who and what kind of woman this is who is touching him—that she is a sinner." Knowing what they were thinking, Jesus turned to one of the Pharisees and said, "Simon, I have something to say to you." Instead of addressing what was on Simon's mind directly, he told him a story about creditors and debtors.

Jesus often used this indirect approach to address the legalistic mind-set of the Pharisees. In Luke 15, Jesus heard the Pharisees and the scribes grumbling and saying, "This fellow welcomes sinners and eats with them." Instead of answering their question of why he ate with sinners, he told them stories—parables. He told them three parables—the lost sheep, the lost coin, and the prodigal son.

In yet another encounter (Lk. 10:25–37; Mt. 22:34–40; Mk. 12:28–34), a lawyer was having a conversation with Jesus about what he must do in order to inherit eternal life. The lawyer concluded with the two great commandments: Love God and love your neighbors. After Jesus commended him for this response, the lawyer asked, "And who is my neighbor?" Here again was the legalistic, exclusive boundary function at work. The assumption behind this question was that there was a prototype of a good neighbor—that of a Jew who followed the law. Jesus again answered a question indirectly, by telling him the parable of the good Samaritan.

By not answering these legalistic and politically charged questions directly, Jesus refused to enter into the dialogue with the same assumptions that the questioners had made. As he told his stories and parables, he stretched the boundaries of the dialogue to include a very different set of assumptions, values, and points of view. In the encounter with Simon, Jesus presented a different way of measuring a person's worth—not by the past reputation of the person, but by the person's present acts of hospitality in response to being forgiven.

> I entered your house; you gave me no water for my feet, but she has bathed my feet with her tears and dried them with her hair. You gave me no kiss, but from the time I came in she has not stopped kissing my feet. You did not anoint my head with oil, but she has anointed my feet with ointment. Therefore, I tell you, her sins, which were many, have been forgiven; hence she has shown great love. But the one to whom little is forgiven, loves little.
>
> *(Luke 7:44–47)*

As he told the parables of the lost sheep, the lost coin, and the prodigal son, Jesus redirected the issue of eating with sinners from an impersonal legalistic approach to a more personal outlook on the situation. He invited the listeners to relate to the sinners as a woman looking for her lost coin, a shepherd searching for his lost sheep, and a loving father welcoming and forgiving his wayward son. He appealed to the experience and compassion of the questioners. He stretched the dialogue boundary from a legal and political arena into a compassionate, relational realm.

In response to the question, Who is my neighbor? Jesus told a parable, popularly known as the parable of the good Samaritan. The story was told from the perspective of a Jew who had fallen on hard times. In the story, he invited the questioner to use a different set of criteria to measure neighborliness. Instead of using a person's ethnic origin, power, and prestige in the religious community as the sole criterion, Jesus invited the lawyer to observe a person's acts of compassion as the more significant measurement—even when these compassionate acts were done by someone like a Samaritan, who did not fit the prototype of what was perceived to be a good neighbor.

In these and other encounters with people with an exclusive attitude, Jesus created a space in which he invited his listeners to step outside their legalistic and political boundaries and consider a different set of assumptions, experiences, relationships, needs, and values. The result of these encounters could disorient the listeners. It could cause the listeners to question their old boundaries and might even enable them to redefine their boundaries. In these encounters Jesus also raised the self-esteem of the one being excluded, such as the woman of the city who was a sinner. Independent of whether the woman was accepted by Simon or not, she was commended for her faithfulness, and she was forgiven.

At this point, I would like to offer a possible definition of the inclusion process based on an examination of and reflection on Jesus' inclusive acts:

> *Inclusion is a discipline of extending our boundary to take into consideration another's needs, interests, experience, and perspective, which will lead to clearer understanding of ourselves and others, fuller description of the issue at hand, and possibly a newly negotiated boundary of the community to which we belong.*

The key to this inclusion process is the facilitation of the extension or stretching of a community's boundary so that there is a time and a space in which to consider other points of view, assumptions, and values. This kind of inclusion process is not unique to the Christian community. However, our Christian faith as manifested through Christ provides us with the

Diagram 4.1: Inclusive Boundary Function

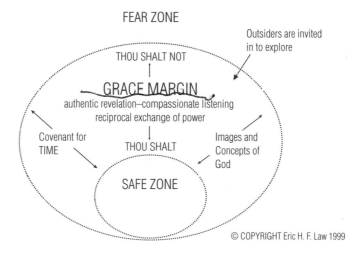

FEAR ZONE

Outsiders are invited
in to explore

THOU SHALT NOT

GRACE MARGIN
authentic revelation–compassionate listening
reciprocal exchange of power

Covenant for
TIME

THOU SHALT

Images and
Concepts of
God

SAFE ZONE

© COPYRIGHT Eric H. F. Law 1999

language to describe this process and the imperative to make it a discipline that we practice as we encounter people who are different.

Diagram 4.1 represents the inclusive boundary function of a Christian community. Notice the only difference between this schematic and the exclusive boundary function as described in diagram 2.1 in chapter 2 is the distance between the safe and fear zones called the "grace margin." Christ invites us to step outside our safe zone and enter the grace margin through his actions, stories, and parables, or through his redirecting of the questions people asked him. Sometimes Christ's invitation to enter the grace margin can be gentle and compassionate; sometimes the invitation can be confusing, if not shocking. But the grace margin keeps us from moving into the fear zone too quickly and making judgments without considering any other perspectives. The grace margin provides time and space for us to maintain an openness to explore—to listen and discover and reflect. In the grace margin, we listen for the Holy Spirit to inspire us, to empower us to speak, and then we listen again. In the grace margin, we acknowledge the abundant grace of God as shown to us by Christ's living, dying, and rising.

How can we enable a community to create such a grace margin? That is the question I would like to answer in the rest of this book. I would like to offer a quick summary of the process here first and then go into details in the following chapters.

1. Drawing an outer parameter

The formation of the grace margin requires an outer parameter beyond which there is still the fear zone. This outer parameter is the conscious extension, even temporarily, of our boundary so that we can consider another's experience and perspective. This extension of our boundary allows us time to reflect and understand the issues as we come face-to-face in the grace margin with others who are different. The outer parameter will keep us safe, even as we are disoriented and confused because we have stepped out of our safe zone. It reminds us of and reaffirms our covenant with God through Christ. It reassures us of the abundant blessing, grace, and love of God. In chapters 5, 6, and 7, I will describe how we can enable a community to draw this outer parameter by contracting for time, arriving at a covenant of what will and will not be addressed in the grace margin, and being faithful to who God is through studying scriptures and sharing the diverse understanding and relationships with God that we all have.

2. Revisiting the boundary of the safe zone

Once the outer parameter is drawn and agreed upon, there is still the need to revisit the safe zone. We must help the community to articulate clearly and consciously the existing safe boundary of the community. Making explicit the safe zone boundary can increase the community's sense of security. If members know from whence they came, they can always find their way back to safety if things do not go well after they have stepped out of their safe zone. This may mean helping them to learn from their history and tradition. In exploring their history, they may discover repeated patterns of exclusion of which they had been unconscious. They may identify who the gatekeepers of their community are. They may learn to articulate what has threatened their sense of security in the past. Not until the community members become conscious of where their safe boundary lies are they able to truly step beyond it into the grace margin. In chapter 8, I will describe some of these models and techniques that can enable a community to clearly understand their own existing safe boundary.

3. Maintaining the grace margin

Having drawn an outer parameter and revisited the safe zone, we create a grace margin. In the grace margin, we invite all parties who have entered to leave behind their legalistic and political approaches to differences and instead focus on the needs, interests, and experiences of one another. In the grace margin, we invite people to share their stories in honest and authentic ways. This is why the previous step of revisiting the safe zone is so important. In the grace margin, we invite people to listen compassionately to one another's revelation. In the grace margin, we strive to maintain a balance of motivation to dialogue, curiosity in learning from each other, and give-and-take of power. My previous two books, *The Wolf Shall Dwell with the Lamb* and *The Bush Was Blazing but Not Consumed,* described many of the techniques and methods for facilitating and maintaining what can happen in the grace margin. Even though the two volumes focus on leading and developing a multicultural community, the methods and techniques are equally applicable to facilitating dialogues across other diversity dimensions—gender, age, ability, sexual orientation, and so on. Most research and models regarding understanding differences, facilitating intercultural communication, resolving conflict across cultures, and so forth, are useful in maintaining the grace margin. In chapter 9, I will enter into a deeper theological discussion of the ministry in the grace margin and then give a summary of some of the skills and techniques needed to facilitate the grace margin.

4. Recreating the community

Having explored the grace margin as a community, we may decide to renegotiate the boundary of the community, although this is not required. The inclusion does not presume the outcome. That is, the inclusion process does not always end with the inclusion of those who challenged the boundary of the community. Sometimes the community, as a result of the inclusion process, may decide to keep its old boundary. Even though the outsiders are still rejected, the difference between this decision and the exclusion boundary function is that in working through the process, we achieve mutual understanding, which may indicate that it is better for the parties involved to remain separate. As a result of working through the inclusion process, a community may reaffirm its identity and mission with a renewed understanding of its core values, or it may redefine itself with new identity and mission. Each time we emerge from the grace margin, we have the potential to become a new creation with a renewed understanding of our covenant in a new context in which we find ourselves. Chapter 10 will explore this process of re-creation of a community as it emerges out of the grace margin.

What I have attempted to do with the short summary above is to organize in a linear fashion the inclusion process so that the readers can get a stronger grasp of the model. (See appendix A—Checklist for Activating the Inclusion Process, which follows this linear model as well.) However, no model can truly capture the reality of how things work out in practice. In reality, some of the steps may need to be reversed. Sometimes we may need to repeat a step before moving on to another step, depending on the readiness of the people involved. The summary here is simply a guide to implementing the inclusion process for a community. We must recognize that any guide we can devise is but an approximation, limited by our human capacity to understand our complex experience. The work of inclusion is not just a human endeavor. It has divine implications, because as we reveal ourselves and our communities' experiences of God to one another, we are participating in the revelation of God. Ultimately, it is Christ who is the true guide to our work of inclusion, because Christ is the gate of our community.

5

He Bent Down and Wrote with His Finger on the Ground

The scribes and the Pharisees brought a woman who had been caught in adultery; and making her stand before all of them, they said to him, "Teacher, this woman was caught in the very act of committing adultery. Now in the law Moses commanded us to stone such women. Now what do you say?" They said this to test him, so that they might have some charge to bring against him. Jesus bent down and wrote with his finger on the ground. When they kept on questioning him, he straightened up and said to them, "Let anyone among you who is without sin be the first to throw a stone at her." And once again he bent down and wrote on the ground. When they heard it, they went away, one by one, beginning with the elders; and Jesus was left alone with the woman standing before him. Jesus straightened up and said to her, "Woman, where are they? Has no one condemned you?" She said, "No one, sir." And Jesus said, "Neither do I condemn you. Go your way, and from now on do not sin again."

John 8:3–11

The scribes and Pharisees were trying to test Jesus by putting him up against a clearly stated Mosaic law in public. They thought surely that if Jesus were one of them, he would follow the law. If he did not, they would use their political power to reject him by bringing up charges against him. They tried to force Jesus to narrow the grace margin in which his compassionate ministry resided. But in his typical fashion, Jesus did not answer their question directly. Instead, he bent down and wrote with his finger on the ground. After some time had passed, he posed a question that presented a different way of seeing the situation. This famous simple question appealed to the accusers' own experience. It invited them to connect with the woman as a person, not as an object to be cast out. Then, bending down again and writing on the ground, he gave more time for people to deal with the situation.

His action provided the first ingredient required to create a grace margin—time for self-examination and reflection. His question invited them to consider what would happen if the law were applied equally to everyone, if everyone who had sinned were to be stoned as well. In doing so, he exposed the accusers' request for the strict application of the law as a political act—meaning that those who had the power were those who enforced the law. Where was the man who committed adultery with her? He was not brought to be punished because, being a man, he had more political influence; therefore, the law was not readily applied to him. In the midst of this emotionally and politically charged situation, Jesus bent down and wrote on the ground, enabling the crowd to find the time to do the kind of reflection required to arrive at a just and compassionate resolution.

Learning to "bend down and write on the ground" is the first step in enabling a community to extend its boundaries to consider another's experience. Community leaders must invite their community to delay making a quick decision that would most likely be based on legal and political maneuvers. Community leaders must be skilled in helping the community contract for more time in creating a grace margin to reconsider the potentially exclusive decision.

In 1997, because of shrinking resources and the transient nature of the neighborhood, a small congregation, which I will call St. Matthew's, decided to explore models of ministries different from the one pastor/one congregation model. In their exploration, members became very excited about a model called "Cluster Ministry," which came out of the experience of the Episcopal Diocese of West Virginia.[1] This model does not require congregations to amalgamate. It only invites the congregations to negotiate a covenant that will allow them to share a leadership team for the purpose of revitalizing the ministries and missions at each one of the church sites. The end result of a cluster leadership team effort could be, for example, four congregations sharing one full-time pastor, one full-time lay administrator, one half-time pastor, and one retired pastor. By sharing a leadership team, the congregations could move out of their financial limitations, which put them in their current survival mode. With the support of the leadership team, the congregations could move forward and look outward in realizing their mission in their own communities.

Having read, digested, and discussed this possibility, St. Matthew's invited four nearby congregations to gather and consider entering into this arrangement. The first meeting was cordial, and the invitees asked a lot of questions. At the second meeting, leaders from only three congregations came. St. Matthew's leaders, noticing the shrinking enthusiasm, asked the other congregations' leaders to decide whether they were willing to participate in this exploration. No definitive answer came from the congregations. Then the dialogue ended. St. Matthew's congregants were a little upset and puzzled, asking, How could they not be excited about this model? But they were determined not to give up.

---

[1] See John H. Smith, *Cluster Ministry—A Faithful Response to Change,* published locally by the Episcopal Diocese of West Virgina in 1997.

With the help of denominational funding, St. Matthew's hosted a conference led by the Right Reverend John H. Smith, bishop of West Virginia, who originated and implemented this model. Again the five congregations involved in the first dialogue meetings, along with other congregations, were invited. At the conference, Bishop Smith was both inspiring and practical. One of the practical insights he offered was that it usually took five years for a cluster to really work. What a relief it was for St. Matthew's to hear that! By forcing a decision at their last exploratory meeting, they had been moving too fast, pushing the other congregations into their fear zones. With that knowledge in mind, St. Matthew's once again invited three other congregations that had representatives at the conference to come together to reconsider becoming a cluster. One of the goals at this initial meeting was to contract for more time so that each congregation could explore this model in more depth before making a decision. As a result, they agreed on the following monthly meeting schedule for the next five months. The first meeting would be a day-long event. The rest of the meetings would be two hours long. At the end of this period, those who wanted to continue the exploration would renegotiate a new covenant for the next period of time.

> **First meeting**—Each congregation would prepare a forty-minute presentation giving a brief history and a description of their present ministries, leadership structure, and mission. They were also invited to share a summary of the strengths, weaknesses, opportunities, and threats to their church.
>
> **Second meeting**—Based on the sharing at their first meeting, they would answer the questions: In what ways could we share that would maximize the ministries at each church? What missions could we share in common and what would be unique to each? What should we not share?
>
> **Third meeting**—At this meeting, they would "get down to business." The discussion topics would be:

What would a Sunday worship schedule be like? What would the leadership structure look like? How would the communications network work? What would be the expectation of the leadership team formed in the new cluster?

Fourth meeting—They would clarify the budget and discuss how the congregational leaders could communicate and educate the members of their church. They would also spend time discussing the denominational implications.

Fifth meeting—They would put together a packet of essential information that they would present to each home congregation.

Sixth meeting—They would draft a two-year covenant, which would be signed by the congregational leaders if their congregations agreed to continue the dialogue about becoming part of the cluster.

Notice the clarity of purpose and time requirement for this process. At the time of my writing this chapter, the four congregations have had their first meeting, in which each congregation shared its history, strengths, struggles, opportunities, and mission directions. At the end of the meeting, those who were present showed a real sense of trust and security. It was expressed in this way, "Even if we don't get to be part of the cluster at the end, the sharing in these meetings would be worth our time." Embedded in the statement is the essence of grace at work—leftovers—and that there is always this extra benefit, independent of the outcome of the negotiations. They knew they were not bound by an expected outcome. Instead, they were excited about the inclusion process that they had begun. They learned to value the time spent exploring in the grace margin because in it they really connected with the abundance of God's given resources and blessing.

The cluster ministry exploration challenged the boundaries of all four congregations involved. In order for them to negotiate graciously and gracefully, they must continue to covenant with one another the time for authentic self-revelation and mutual listening—sharing and understanding experiences, needs, interests, and missions.

In 1998 the Anglican Diocese of New Westminster in British Columbia, like many of the denominations at the time, was struggling with the issue of whether to allow blessings of same-sex unions in the church. At the Diocesan Synod, an annual gathering of delegates from the eighty congregations in the diocese, a motion was put forth asking the synod to allow the bishop to give permission for clergy to bless same-sex couples who wished to have their relationship affirmed in their church community. This represented a major challenge to the comfortable boundary of the Anglican Church. In fact, none of the Canadian dioceses had approved anything like it.

After the motion was presented and seconded, the bishop, who chairs the Diocesan Synod, gave an impassioned speech to invite the delegates to debate this issue with respect and civility and to listen diligently to both sides of the argument. Furthermore, he conditioned the debate by inviting those who were for and against the motion to speak alternately, allowing both sides equal opportunity to address their concerns. After more than two hours of debate, the exhausted synod took a vote, and the result was 159 votes for and 150 votes against. Legally the motion passed, because decisions require only a simple majority vote. But in order for a motion to carry, the bishop had to consent to it. The bishop then told the delegates that he would not give his consent until he had consulted with other appropriate bodies of the Anglican Church of Canada. This caused a wave of mixed emotions from the delegates. Six months later, he issued a statement that outlined the following five-point plan of action for the next two years:

1. The creation of a Bishop's Commission on Gay and Lesbian Voices to help parishes understand the experiences of gay and lesbian Christians

2. The "twinning" of parishes within the diocese for intentional discussion and study on same-sex unions

3. The creation of a Commission on Faith and Doctrine to prepare short study papers on biblical and ethical issues raised by same-sex unions for use in parish study groups

4. The establishment of a Canonical and Legal Commission to determine whether there are existing impediments under Canadian or church law to prevent a bishop from authorizing the blessing of same-sex unions

5. The preparation of a rite of blessing that could be used if same-sex blessings were approved in 2001

The bishop knew that this boundary negotiation could not be done through the legal and political process, which left little room for grace. Both sides were very emotional about the issue, and the vote count was too close. Having recognized that, he decided to contract with the diocese for a "grace" period of two years to further discuss this issue. In this time period, there would be opportunities for the people of the diocese to consider the issue—not in a political arena, but in a community-oriented and respectful environment. The different commissions he had set up were attempts to create a level playing field on which there would be a balance of power, listening, and revelation. In the Annual Synod 2001, a vote will be taken again on this issue. Of course, people from both sides were complaining and questioning. What they did not know was that the bishop was bending down and writing on the ground.

Whenever a community's boundary is challenged, we need to help the community avoid making a quick decision that is often based on political and legal maneuvers, resulting in exclusion. The best way to do so is to covenant with the community for the appropriate amount of time needed to explore the issues with greater understanding before a decision can be made. The purpose of the grace period is not to avoid the issue by delaying the inevitable conflict. Therefore, it is very important to state clearly the covenanted time allotted. In both examples I described above, the purposes and goals of the grace period were clearly defined. More importantly, the covenants also clearly stated the time commitment required for community members to enter into a grace margin with ease and security.

In general, a community that has learned to act inclusively when its boundary is challenged has regular covenanted time to explore different issues. "Practice makes perfect" is a good motto to remember. Here are a few examples of regular covenanted time that many Christian communities have adopted:

1. A congregation in an ethnically diverse neighborhood schedules quarterly cultural celebrations. At each celebration, three or four ethnic, cultural, or age groups in the parish are invited to share with the congregation ways in which they are different and the important things that the rest of the congregation needs to know about them in order for them to feel included.

2. A congregation builds into its regular annual schedule a biannual listen-in of the neighborhood community, in which neighborhood leaders and groups are invited to share what they see as the needs and concerns in the neighborhood.

3. Congregations with denominational affiliation have many opportunities to enter into explorations regularly by participating in annual denomination-sponsored events such as intercongregational dialogue, diversity training, antiracism programs, and so on.

4. A congregation invites its members to participate in regional interdenominational and interfaith dialogue events on a regular basis.

These regularly contracted times for exploration at the edge of our boundaries is crucial to the health of a faith community. It prevents the community from becoming too comfortable and content inside its safe zone. Such contentment may lead to the tightening up of the community's boundary function. Setting aside time to enter into the grace margin periodically will enable a community to continue to be relevant and responsive to the needs of the people in the wider community. These experiences in the grace margin will enable a community to react more inclusively when its boundary is being challenged. Its members will know it takes time to really extend their boundary to consider and understand another's reality. They will know to withhold their judgment and covenant the appropriate amount of time for further exploration and reflection. They will also know that working in the grace margin is a worthy thing to do, independent of the outcome of the exploration. They will know to imitate Jesus by bending down and writing on the ground, allowing time for constructive questioning, self-examination, and reflection.

6

Thou Shalt and Thou Shalt Not...

In the last chapter we explored the first step to activating the inclusion process—making time for grace. In this chapter we will explore how to enable a community to consciously extend its boundary by drawing an outer boundary and thereby creating room for the grace that is necessary for the inclusion process.

> You shall have no other gods before me. You shall not make for yourself an idol... You shall not make wrongful use of the name of the LORD your God... Remember the sabbath day, and keep it holy... Honor your father and your mother... You shall not murder. You shall not commit adultery. You shall not steal. You shall not bear false witness against your neighbor. You shall not covet your neighbor's house; you shall not covet your neighbor's wife...
>
> *Exodus 20:3–17*

In the story of the exodus, God, through Moses led the Israelites out of Egypt, "out of the house of slavery." On the one hand, the liberation from slavery must have created great excitement—being free at last! On the other hand, with this

59

freedom came the physical and spiritual wandering in the wilderness. Slavery, as oppressive as it was, was still a safe zone for the Israelites, because it was the only reality they knew. In slavery, they were governed by their masters and mistresses, who made decisions and set rules for them. When they stepped out of their safe zone into freedom in the wilderness, they had to leave that structured life behind. How could they live as a free people now? What would be the new rules, and who would set them? Many a time they entered into their fear zone and complained to Moses, "It would have been better for us to serve the Egyptians than to die in the wilderness" (Ex. 14: 12).

God responded to their fear and confusion with the covenant, which begins with the Ten Commandments, as we popularly call them. The covenant was the outer parameter keeping the Israelites from stepping into their fear zone and, therefore, enabling them to explore and live as a free people in the abundant grace of God. This outer parameter, the covenant, was not the same as the oppressive rules that they were accustomed to as slaves. In the wilderness, where there was uncertainty about their internal governance and their future, the covenant articulated the relationship between the Israelites and God—they would have no idols, and they would keep their Sabbath and worship God regularly. The covenant also prescribed the behavior required for them to live together as a free people without pushing each other into the fear zone—what they should and should not do in order to uphold the balance of the new community. They will not kill. They will honor their mothers and fathers. They will not steal. They will not steal another man's wife in this community, and so forth. This behavioral covenant provided the safety they needed to learn to live as a free people under one God. The drawing of the outer parameter, the covenant, turned the fearful wilderness into a grace margin in which they learned to trust God, who would provide them with streams of flowing water and manna from heaven.

The inclusion process requires a community to step outside its safe zone. This prospect can cause people to fear that once they step outside their safe boundary, there will be no boundary left. They will be left with no solid ground to stand on. They will not know what is right or wrong anymore. They will be in the wilderness. They may fear that their whole community will disintegrate. To activate the inclusion process, we must learn to help our communities draw an outer parameter by negotiating a behavioral covenant that describes the respectful grace-filled relationship among the parties involved —turning the wilderness into a grace margin.

In consulting with the staff of a large church, I developed a plan to invite everyone to share their experiences of working in the office, both positive and negative, and then as a group to set goals and design an action plan that would address constructively the issues that they had identified. After I presented the process, the treasurer said, "We can't do that! What if someone decided that he should have a raise? What if people decided that everyone should have a three-month paid vacation?"

"I agree," another senior staff member said, "We can't have everybody making decisions that should be made by the people in the management of the organization."

I could feel the frustration level rising from the rest of the staff. Their body language said, "Why bother trying to be inclusive!" It was apparent that what was said was interpreted as an act of exclusion. The grace margin I was trying to establish was being squeezed narrower by the vested power and legalistic responses of the senior members of the staff. I was on the verge of losing this group.

My response: "I think those are important questions to ask. As we move forward, we need to draw some parameters for the work that we are doing in the consultation. What would be the appropriate parameter within which we should do our work?"

After some discussion, the group reaffirmed that the purpose of the consultation was to improve the working relationship and communication in the office and that the group would not deal with policy and personnel issues. Any concerns that came out of the consultation regarding personnel would be referred to the appropriate bodies in the organization. With that, the whole group agreed to move forward.

The first step in drawing the outer parameter is to name the fear of the community. Having acknowledged the fear-zone boundary, we pull the community gently into the grace margin by stating what we will *not* do. The danger here is that we may pull too far back and allow the community to retreat deep within its safe zone, where there is little room for change and exploration. Therefore, the pulling back from the fear zone must be accompanied by the pushing out from the safe zone.

St. Paul's was a congregation that had suffered a major decline in past years and was financially unable to support a full-time pastor. The judicatory leaders had been talking about reshaping the ministry configuration in terms of the number of congregations in that geographical area. I was charged with helping the congregation explore a realistic and faithful course for its future direction. I knew rumors abounded that St. Paul's was no longer viable and, therefore, should be closed and the property liquidated to support the other congregations in the area, which were supposedly in less trouble. With that rumor I had no choice but to include closure as an option as we negotiated the outer parameter for our consultation.

Members of St. Paul's did not like the idea when I first brought it up. We struggled with it for two meetings in which I reiterated that I was not there to close their church, but rather to help them explore all the options as faithfully as possible. For the exploration to be meaningful, closure had to be part of the dialogue. Finally the parish leaders agreed to let closure be one of five options that they would consider. As a result, the exploration of their future options was much more fruitful because congregation members, even though they were a little apprehensive, were able to deal with their issues with honesty and clarity. With the support of a grace-filled environment, St. Paul's faced death head–on and emerged with a new identity and new energy for mission. Working through the grace margin, they discovered resurrection. If we had not included closure as one of the discussion items, the rumor of closure would have created more fear and denial, destroying any chance for extending their boundary to consider new forms of ministries.

To help a community draw an outer parameter, we must work with the tension between stretching the boundary too far, which will push the community into the fear zone, and not stretching it far enough, being too safe. If we are too timid in drawing this outer boundary, fearing that we will push the community into the fear zone, the community may not extend its boundary far enough to allow for meaningful, constructive exploration. If we are too anxious to get things moving and push too far, the community may shut down, returning to its tightly guarded safe zone. For this process to work, we must spend a substantial amount of time negotiating this outer parameter until all the key players agree on a grace margin that is not too fearful, but not too safe. This requires gentle pushing and pulling, deliberate truth-telling, clear use of language in terms of what we will and will not do, and, most importantly, patience.

Here are a couple of examples of setting an outer parameter that I have come across in different contexts:

1. I was watching a documentary on PBS called "It's Elementary," which was about the struggle of teachers trying to teach a curriculum that includes gay and lesbian issues to elementary school children. At one point in the program, two guest speakers, a woman and a man, were addressing a class. The woman said, "I am not here to make you gay. I am just here to share my experience as a lesbian. You don't have to agree with me. But I do expect you to at least listen and understand..."

2. In an interreligious dialogue program, one of the outer parameters expressed as part of the ground rules for dialogue was: We are not here to convert the others to our faith. We are here to listen to each other so that we can

gain a better understanding of each other's beliefs and values.

In both these examples, the participants were clear about what they would and would not do. I make it a discipline to present a set of Respectful Community Guidelines[1] at the beginning of every meeting.

R = take RESPONSIBILITY for what you say and feel without blaming others.

E = engage in EMPATHETIC listening.

S = be SENSITIVE to differences in communication styles.

P = PONDER what you hear and feel before you speak.

E = EXAMINE your own assumptions and perceptions.

C = keep CONFIDENTIALITY.

T = TOLERATE ambiguity because we are *not* here to debate who or what is right or wrong.

This set of guidelines is a behavioral covenant that I invite the people at the meeting to discuss, digest, and affirm. It again states what we will and will not do in the meeting. These guidelines address the fear of people's blaming, debating, and not keeping confidentiality. They also encourage people to listen, ponder, self-examine, and be sensitive to one another. These are not laws that we enforce, but a description of the relationship of the people involved for the sake of building the community.

When a group meets for the first time, facilitating a dialogue on inclusion and respect can help the newly formed community discover the beginning of a behavioral covenant. Here is the list of questions I work through with the group:

---

[1]For a fuller description of how to help a community affirm such guidelines, see Eric H. F. Law, *The Bush Was Blazing but Not Consumed* (St. Louis: Chalice Press, 1996), 83–87.

1. What do others need to know about me/us in order for me/us to function effectively in this gathering?
2. How do I know I am being included?
3. How do I know I am being respected?
4. Based on answers I hear from others and my own answers to the above three questions, what are my/our responsibilities in making the gathering inclusive and respectful of everyone?
5. What are the community ground rules that we need to affirm before we start our work? What will we do? What will we not do?

Sometimes it is appropriate to invite the community to arrive at its own covenant, especially when the boundary challenge is coming from within, where one group in the community feels excluded. For this purpose, I have designed a process called "Rights, Respect, and Responsibilities"[2] (see appendix B for the full description of the process). In this process, community members are invited to explore the following three topics:

1. Rights—What are the rights of people in this community?
2. Respect—What does respect mean for the different groups and individuals in the community?
3. Responsibilities—What are the responsibilities of each individual in upholding one another's rights and respecting each person in the community?

---

[2]I got the idea for the process while listening to a lecture given by Charles C. Hayes, the executive director of First Liberty Institute at George Mason University, in 1993 on Religious Freedom in America, in which he talked about the "Three Rs" of religious liberty. See also Michael D. Cassity, Os Guinness, Charles C. Haynes, John Seel, Timothy L. Smith, and Oliver S. Thomas, *Living with Our Deepest Differences—Religious Liberty in a Pluralistic Society* (Boston: Learning Connections Publishers, 1990), 13.

At the end of the process, community members are invited to write down what they think should be included as part of a list of community principles that the whole community should uphold. These suggestions are then collected, collated, and summarized into a set of community ground rules to be published, shared, and reaffirmed every time the community gathers.

In general, an inclusive community has a community covenant, in a form similar to the Respectful Communication Guidelines, that its members reaffirm regularly in their meetings or gatherings, stating in general terms what they will and will not do to uphold a constructive, respectful community life together. Sometimes when we least expect it, a controversial issue pops up, and it is too late to reaffirm any respectful communication guidelines. Therefore, an inclusive community makes it a discipline to present and affirm the community covenant at each event, whether it is a meeting on a finance matter, a Bible study group, a youth group, an intercultural dialogue, or a similar meeting. When such a community's boundary is being challenged, its members will know now to covenant with each other and the "outsiders" to explore and learn in a respectful, relationally focused environment. Such a community will not enter the wilderness in fear. Instead, they will welcome the exile, trusting in God's abundant grace and trusting in one another through the covenant they have made, thereby turning the wilderness into a place of grace where there are life-giving flowing streams and manna from heaven.

'Twas grace that taught my heart to fear,

and grace my fears relieved;

how precious did that grace appear

the hour I first believed!

John Newton (1725–1807)

7

You Shall Have No Other Gods
before Me

"What was the attitude of God in the creation story?" I asked a group of people in a Bible study group after we read Genesis 1.[1]

"What do you mean?" a participant asked, as if he had never thought of such a thing as "the attitude of God."

"How does God feel about the different things that God has created?" I replied. "Read the text in front of you; what can you decipher?"

They read the text again, still puzzled by my questions. Someone said, "That they were good?"

"Yes, but more precisely." I decided to be more directed in my questioning. "What was God's attitude toward light?"

"That the light was good."

"What was God's attitude toward darkness?"

There was a pregnant silence. "It doesn't say" was one of the replies.

---

[1] I am indebted to Walter Wink, from whom I learned to use this line of questions to study Genesis 1.

"Did God say that darkness is bad, and therefore God created light?"

"No."

"But how many of you assumed when you read this passage that darkness was undesirable?" I asked. Almost everyone raised a hand. "If you read the rest of chapter 1 of Genesis, God is quite neutral about the diversity of things that were created, even when they seem to us to be opposites—day and night, earth and sky, sea and dry land, man and woman."

This is a typical dialogue I use when facilitating a biblical reflection on the topic of diversity and inclusion. When we realize that it is not God who makes judgments about what is good or bad in the diversity of creation, we confront the fact that it is we who make the assumption that one thing is better than another. It is we—not God—who exclude the things that we consider to be bad and to be feared (and therefore undesirable). But we want to make God think the way we do. We want God to have the same categories of what is good and bad, right and wrong. If we love someone, God must love that person. If we hate someone, God must hate that person too. We confine God to our limited way of seeing and perceiving the world. In the name of our limited, incomplete image of God, we have sinned greatly in the past. With the image of God as exclusively a white male figure, we jumped to the conclusion—most often unconsciously—that people who were not white and male were inferior or less than the divine race or gender. With that conclusion, we waged war against those who did not fit our image of God. We even implemented programs of genocide against them; we kept people in slavery because they did not fit our image of God.

For the Christian community, many acts of exclusion can be traced to the sin of idolatry. Knowing only our limited, incomplete concept of God, we assume that we know all there is to know about God. We create an idol based on these limited ideas, and we worship it. We hold our idol up as the only god and measure others' worth with it. For religious people, inclusion is not only an interpersonal issue but also a theological one. As we take the time to consider another's reality, we must make room for the different images and concepts of God that the other brings. In doing so, we discover the different faces of the same God. Instead of confining God and making God look and act like us, we attempt to gain a greater vision of who God is. We acknowledge that God is greater than you and me and everything we know combined. We accept that God's creation, action, and purpose are beyond our comprehension. In the grace margin, we must know God for who God is—not for what we want God to be for us.

Jesus' ministry, at its core, reshaped and extended people's boundaries regarding their perceptions of God. The religious leaders of the time took the Mosaic covenant, which was supposed to describe the dynamic relationship between God and the Israelites, and fossilized it into a static set of laws. The image of God that religious leaders like the scribes and Pharisees used was that of a judge applying the law to measure each person's worth, without regard for the relationships or context in which people lived. After pointing out this exclusive boundary function, which had little room for grace, Jesus drew an outer parameter that distilled the complicated labyrinth of laws into two commandments that focused on the relational—love God and love your neighbors as yourself. The refocusing of the covenant stretched the boundary function of the religious community from a legalistic, behavior-based operation to a relational, contextual process. By doing so, Jesus created a grace margin in which he could exercise his compassionate ministry.

To make room for grace, Jesus referred to God as "Father," which has become one of the most dominant images of God in the two thousand years of Christian history. The parenthood of God had appeared in the Hebrew Scriptures but was not the predominant image of God. The compassion of God as presented by Jesus is not so much that of a judge or a king, but of a parent who has personal knowledge of the struggle and experience of his or her children. By emphasizing the father image of God, Jesus attempted to balance the overly legalistic view of the religious leaders of the time. The compassionate spirit of the parent-God concept enabled Jesus and his followers to include many people whom the religious establishment of the time would exclude—the unclean, tax collectors, prostitutes, Gentiles, Samaritans, and women. Jesus, being fully human, allows God to be truly compassionate to us. God through Jesus Christ has personal knowledge of humanity in all its facets, and therefore God can truly claim to be our parent. Therefore, we, through Jesus Christ, can be secured as sons and daughters of God. This personal connection with God through Jesus has a number of consequences:

1. If we are all sons and daughters of God, that makes us all siblings. What happens when we disagree? We can no longer claim that God is on our side only, because the same argument is being made by the people on the other side who are our brothers and sisters in God's family. I often wonder what football teams pray for at the beginning of their games. I wonder if both teams pray for the same thing—to win. I wonder how God will answer their prayers. For children of God, either-or and winner-loser solutions to our differences are no longer acceptable. Like a parent trying to teach children that winning is not everything, God challenges us to work out our differences in a brotherly and sisterly way.

2. As children of God, we move through a process of maturity in faith. Parents set down many rules for their children when the children are young. But as their children grow older, parents begin to let them accept responsibilities for themselves. As this process continues, the rules become more flexible. The relationship can be transformed from a children-must-follow-the-rules one to a mature, respectful relationship between adults. How

would this continuation of the parent–child relationship inform us of our relationship with a parent–God?

3. As children, we can effect change in the rules set by our parent–God. How radical to think that we can change God's mind! As children, many of us were masters at plucking the heartstrings of our parents to get what we wanted. Why not God then, if God is like a parent to us? A scriptural example of this is the story of the Canaanite woman's changing Jesus' mind regarding who was included in God's salvation. In the covenant through Jesus Christ, our relationship is no longer a one-way street, where God gives us the law and we follow it. In this covenant through Jesus, God reveals God's self to us, and we reveal ourselves to God. We change in response to God's grace, and God changes in response to our faithfulness and needs.

Through Christ, our relationships with God and with one another are anchored in the compassionate love of a parent–God. In that love, rules, laws, and traditions are upheld only when they support this organic, dynamic relationship with God. Time and again, rather then follow the letter of the law, Jesus and his disciples broke the law in the name of upholding this relationship with God. Christ pushes us out of our safe zone of rules and traditions into the grace margin, where there is room to explore, learn, and negotiate with others, even with God.

While acknowledging how radical and central the father image of God was for Jesus' time and for the early church, I also must confess that in writing the previous paragraphs I have avoided using the word *father* as much as possible. Instead, I used the word *parent*. I am sure that Jesus must have had a very good relationship with his human father, Joseph. And the father image for God is a meaningful one for those of us who grew up with very good relationships with our fathers. But for me and for many people I know, the concept of a father–God is a difficult one with which to connect. By the time I was born, the youngest of six children, my father seemed to have lost interest in children. I do not remember a time when my father held me. Father was someone whom I asked for permission to go on a field trip. Father was someone who signed my report card. Father was someone to whom I related through my mother. Based only on what I knew about my father, I formed an image of God as a distant, detached authority figure. I later found out that my concept of a God modeled after my father was very far from the original intent of Jesus' concept of the Father. I had committed idolatry by limiting God according to only what I knew.

When I was in college in the '70s, while participating in a weekly Bible study group, I discovered images of God as feminine, and specifically as a mother. To my surprise, these images were there in the Bible—the mother eagle, the Spirit and Wisdom as the feminine, and so forth. My eyes were opened in one study session when the facilitator invited us to imagine the voice of God at Jesus' baptism as the voice of a woman after giving birth. In this enlightening moment, my "theology" came into place. Yes, God had been present to me like my mother, who was always there for me, advising, nurturing, encouraging, and loving me. Like my mother, who forced me to maintain my family ties, God forces me to maintain my ties to the human family. I could see the face of God as I recalled my mother praying after receiving communion, or being at my bedside when I was sick. The things I had been feeling all these years that were of God became real to me, all because someone included the image of God as a mother and shared it with me.

The inclusion of the mother image of God allowed me to include the feminine side of myself as part of what God has given me. It allowed me to accept that side of myself that society considered feminine and, to my mind then, not godly. It allowed me to be whole. The mother–God image invited me to see and perceive the role of women with new eyes. It allowed me to appreciate and support the women's movement of the church. As my boundary was extended to include a different image of God, I became more gracious and accepting of who I was, and I became more open to meeting, listening, and learning from others who had a different perception and experience. Although I was delighted with this discovery, I had to be careful not to take it to the extreme and become idolatrous again by making God exclusively female, for then I would be doing what I did with the father-God image earlier in my life—limiting God.

There is something about humankind that keeps wanting to limit God based only on our own limited experience. Sometimes we even take the grace margin that Jesus created by emphasizing the personal relationship with God and unconsciously narrow it by turning it into a legalistic, exclusive, tight boundary. We make our personal relationship with God into an idol, a private God for us alone, which therefore excludes others who do not have the exact same way of relating to God. Back in the '70s again, when I was going to college, almost every day when I walked across the campus, someone would ask if I were saved. If I stopped and talked with this person, he or she would ask, "Do you have a personal relationship with Jesus?" My answer to this question was, and still is, "Yes." When I had time, I would talk to this person about how God had helped me through many hard times in my life, how God was present to me also in the worship traditions of the different church denominations and how God had given me the gift to think and reason in order to understand the world. Then I usually invited that person to worship with me in the Episcopal church on campus. By this time, this person's face wore a puzzled look—a look that said, How could God be all those things? Soon I knew the dialogue would end and that I would be judged by this person as not yet being saved because I had not been saved in the specific way that this person had experienced salvation. I did not cite a particular time and place in which I was born again and accepted Jesus Christ as my personal savior.

All the questions that this person asked me stemmed from very significant concepts of God, based on scriptures and the tradition of the church. But if these concepts are the only ones we use to describe our relationship with God, excluding all others, we have made an idol that we worship. When we exclusively use a personal relationship with God through Christ as the only legitimate relationship with God, we are abusing what Christ was trying to do in the first place. His ministry sought to expand the repertoire of images and attributes of God, of which the personal relationship with God is but one. His emphasis on our being the children of God did not eliminate other ways of relating to the fullness of God. God still judges us. God still gets angry at us. God still laments for us. God still gets jealous when we commit idolatry. God still requires us to follow commandments. Jesus simply anchored all these different faces of God onto the grace, love, and generosity of a compassionate parent-God. If we simply apply the personal relationship as the only rule to measure everyone's worthiness as a member of God's community, we are no more than the Pharisees and scribes that Jesus challenged in his time.

Scripture provides a record of God's diverse relationships with humanity—through the patriarchs and matriarchs; Moses and the exodus events; the prophets; Christ in his earthly relationship with humanity, his suffering, death, and resurrection; and then through the acts of the community of early believers. In these records are a wealth of imageries and concepts of God and of Jesus Christ that constantly challenge our limited perception of God. God's image shifts from time to time, depending on where and who we are. The rich are challenged by a different image of God than are the poor. Women relate to a different set of images of God than do men. A scientist's relationship with God may be very different from that of a poet. The minute we think we have God figured out, there it is, another image that does not quite fit, and so we have to work on relating to others and to God in new ways again. When we are faithful in studying and experiencing these diverse images and concepts of God and of Christ, we move away from the danger of idolatry.

In the formation of the early church, various communities had different records of Jesus' ministry. When they were accepted by the early church council as part of the canon that formed what is now known as the New Testament, the early church leaders included four versions of the gospel story with very different depictions of Jesus. Each gospel story expressed a theology relevant to the community from which the text emerged. There were many similarities, and, more importantly, there were many discrepancies, such as the sequence of events, contradictions of facts, variations of the same incidents, and so on. David Rhoads described this in his book *The Challenge of Diversity:*

> Each New Testament writing tends to draw a line of judgment whereby those who have chosen the good way are on one side and those who have chosen the evil way are on the other side. However, the New Testament writings as a collection relativize the absoluteness of each individual writing, because together the writings draw the line of judgment at so many different places!...Paul draws the line over the issue of faith in God's justification by grace, Mark over the willingness to relinquish self for the good news, Matthew over the righteous fulfilling of the Law, Luke over the merciful commitment to the poor, and John over the spiritual knowing of God....Thus, the canon leads us to shift from a limited either-or mentality to a both-and mentality in the larger embrace of God's wisdom.[2]

The agreement to include these different points of view in the Bible had to be made with grace. Each community apparently did not insist that its version of Christ's story was

[2]David Rhoads, *The Challenge of Diversity—The Witness of Paul and the Gospels* (Minneapolis: Fortress Press, 1996), 140.

the only correct one, excluding all others. I have no illusion that the church leaders at the time did not use their power and various legal maneuverings to get their ways in that discussion, which formulated the current collection of texts. However, I am extremely grateful for the resulting scriptures, which I believe have maintained a margin of grace for interpreters in the last two thousand years. As we struggle with the discrepancies, opposing viewpoints, and diverse styles of writing, we are invited to explore and understand the early Christian communities' different contexts and their specific relationships with God through Christ. The authority of the Christian scriptures demands that we rise above the specific images or concepts as presented by the different personalities and communities and see the greater, not readily discernible, true Christ, who, despite all the writings that have tried to describe him, is still a mystery. We relate to Christ not as a static historic figure, but as a living presence among us, interacting with each of us differently according to our unique context and experience. The authority of the Christian scriptures as a collection demands grace from us as we read them day after day, week after week, year after year.

For three years I worked as the congregational development officer of an Anglican diocese with eighty congregations. On many occasions, the congregation with which I was working faced issues of inclusion. How do we include the people in our neighborhood? How can we include more youth in our midst? The average age of our congregation is getting older each year. How do we include more contemporary music in our liturgy so that young people will feel more welcome? But we don't want to exclude the old-timers who really love the traditional music. What should we do about the request from a lesbian couple who want our pastor to bless their relationship? The changes in demographics around the congregation had challenged its boundary. The temptation was for the group to fall back on a simple, exclusive boundary function in dealing with these changes, narrowing the margin of grace.

In order to maintain the grace margin within which I could work with these congregations, I made it a discipline to study scripture at the beginning of every meeting. I usually chose the gospel reading of the upcoming Sunday worship. After doing it for a while, I began to see the power of scriptures to help congregations focus on matters that they needed to address from a theological as well as practical perspective. By studying scriptures together, the community was invited to relate to God as a living entity, not as a static set of rules. The images and concepts of God presented in the scriptures allowed the community to reconnect with a side of God that might not have readily come to mind for them. Embedded in the scriptural passages were many empowering, affirming, challenging, and sometimes surprising images and concepts of God and Christ. When I enabled the community to connect with these wonderful, life-giving images, the community came alive as well.

A church in an urban setting was exploring calling a new priest. The neighborhood had changed in the previous years to include a large population of low-income immigrants. The previous priest had implemented a number of successful social outreach programs, which, on the one hand, had support from many of the younger members but, on the other hand, had met with complaints and resistance from some of the long-time members. I facilitated a day-long process to help them discern a direction for their church and the kind of priest they would seek. As I always did, I started the day with studying the gospel lesson from the upcoming Sunday liturgy. It so happened that the passage was popularly known as "the dishonest steward" (Lk. 16:1–13)— a text that has caused many priests and pastors great pain in their efforts to interpret and create a sermon from it. The question I posed was, How does this passage inform or connect with our work today? As the small groups discussed this passage, they were puzzled. One person asked, "Why did you choose this passage to study today?" I explained that it was one of the scriptural lessons of the upcoming Sunday. They were puzzled about Jesus' actions. How could Jesus compliment a dishonest person? That did not fit their image of Jesus at all. As the group continued to struggle with the passage, one person stood up and said, "I'm really confused."

"Maybe Jesus meant to confuse us!" someone else said. They all laughed. Then a moment of serious reflection set in. Maybe God wanted us to be confused. That was exactly where they were. They were confused about the direction they were going. They were confused about the different emotions that they felt about the new outreach programs implemented by the last priest. One group used the departure of the priest as an opportunity to push the church back to its old safe zone. "Let us hire a pastor who will bring us back to the good old days when we didn't have strangers hanging around the church all the time." Another group wanted a new leader who would continue the ministries started by the last priest. "We must continue what we started, or we will surely cease to be a viable ministry for God in this neighborhood." One of the assumptions on both sides was that as Christians, they were supposed to know what was right or wrong. There ought to be no confusion about things at all. With that in mind, they argued and debated about what kind of priest they would want. The community was becoming more and more polarized.

The statement "Maybe Jesus meant to confuse us!" broke open this narrow margin. It presented a new image of Christ, even though it might not have been the intent of the writer of the gospel. But in the context of this community, God inspired this group of people to connect with God in a different way. Confusion, which was something unacceptable to them before, was now all right. The acceptance of confusion allowed them to dialogue without making judgments about each other. Therefore, they were better able to include and even to accept the other's point of view. As we moved on with the day's process, exploring where they had been and where they were now, they recognized that they had reached a very uncertain point in the life of the community. At the end of the day, the community agreed that instead of moving immediately to call a new priest, which required them to know who they were and what they wanted to be, they would move into a full year of intentional interim ministry. As a community, they covenanted for a period of time in which they could work through their confusion. They withheld their decision making until they could explore their differences in the grace margin.

Scriptural passages are like the DNA pattern of a human being. We are discovering a lot of things about our DNA in medical research, but we still do not fully comprehend how the diverse individuals of the human family are created from the DNA pattern. In the same way, each Bible passage shows a different side of God. Each passage shows a different relationship that God has with different people. No single image or concept in a passage presents the whole picture of God. It is in the discipline of reading and learning from the different parts of the scriptures that we begin to see the bigger idea of who God is. Even then, we do not know the full mystery of God. Perhaps this is what it means for us to say that scriptures contain all things necessary for salvation, but we still do not know the full extent of how this process works. But it works—that is the mystery. When we study scriptures faithfully, new life emerges. When we are open to the Holy Spirit as we study the scriptures together, God will find a way to connect with us, to make God's presence known to us, and to provide an outer safe parameter in which we can extend our boundary to consider who we are, who others are, and who God is.

When a community studies scriptures in the grace margin, God becomes a living player in the exploration and dialogue. We do not ask, What do we want? but, What does God want? Including God in the grace margin removes the issues from a purely personal human endeavor and places them in the divine realm. It moves us beyond our need to be powerful or to be right. It turns us to God and invites us to see how God through Christ will mediate, appreciate, and even embrace our differences. Instead of asking, What does it require for a person to be included in our community? we ask, What does God require us to do to meet the needs of those who come into our midst? Instead of asking, Do we have enough to let another in? we ask, How can we be gracious in sharing the abundance of God's love, blessing, and grace?

Besides studying scriptures regularly, an inclusive community makes it a discipline to present a variety of concepts and images of Christ and God whenever it is appropriate, especially when these images are connected with the scriptural readings of the seasons of the church. The following is a list of possible opportunities to do this:

1. Preachers and Sunday school teachers of the community can take advantage of the wealth of God images in our scriptures and present them to the community through their ministries of preaching and teaching.

2. Intercessors can utilize a wealth of images of God in formulating their public prayers. The diversity of God images will invite the diverse community members to better connect with the corporate prayer life.

3. Music ministers can intentionally select music with lyrics that enable the community to connect with a diversity of God images and concepts.

4. Our church buildings and our homes can have visual art that presents a diversity of images of Christ and of God.

5. Leaders can help ministry groups in the community discover and articulate their driving images of God. The community should also provide a time and space for them to share their "theologies" with one another in a respectful, mutually supportive environment.

6. A community can regularly reaffirm its baptismal covenant to remind everyone of the dynamic relationship they have with God through Christ.

A community that consistently presents and affirms the variety of images and concepts of God is more likely to act inclusively when its boundary is being challenged. When members of such a community encounter another who has a different relationship with God, they are less likely to judge and exclude the other. Instead, since they have been accustomed to exploring a wealth of images of God with others in their own community, they can move with ease into the grace margin to consider another's experience with God without judgment. The work of inclusion ultimately is an act of our faithfulness to God. By practicing a discipline of inclusion when our boundary is challenged, we recognize our limited perception of God each time and know, therefore, to avoid making an idol for ourselves. Instead, we welcome the opportunity to enter the grace margin to learn more about God.

Day by day,
O dear Lord, three things I pray:
To see thee more clearly,
Love thee more dearly, and
Follow thee more nearly
Day by day...

Attributed to Richard of Chichester (1197–1253)

8

The Gatekeeper Opens
the Gate for Christ

In the last three chapters, I have described the three major components for facilitating a community's extension of its boundary: covenanting for more time, enabling its members to articulate what they will and will not do in their use of that time, and studying and raising up a variety of images and concepts of God. Through these processes, a grace margin is created. Some communities still require one more step before they are ready to engage the insiders and the outsiders in mutual revelation, listening, and understanding within the grace margin. In order to truly step out of their safe zone, community members must know what their safe zone is and where its boundary lies. More importantly, they need to know who or what is controlling their community's boundary.

> The gatekeeper opens the gate for [the shepherd], and the sheep hear his voice. He calls his own sheep by name and leads them out.
>
> *John 10:3*

Who are the gatekeepers in a community? Who controls the boundary function of a community? Christ the Good

Shepherd cannot lead us out of our safe zone into the grace margin unless the gatekeepers of our community let Christ through the gate first. Unless the gatekeepers of a community are willing to relinquish control of the gate, Christ cannot be the gate, and we will have little room for the grace margin. This step of revisiting the safe zone is especially important for communities that have not done much self-examination in the past.

"I don't know why the bishop sent you here. We have no problem. We are a loving, caring, welcoming church," a congregation leader said, challenging my presence in their midst. I did not respond to the complaint directly; I needed to contract with them for some time and to find more room for the grace margin first. So I said, "As long as I am here, why don't we at least use the time to study scripture together and for you to tell me what's been happening at your church these days." I presented the Respectful Communication Guidelines. We studied the gospel reading of the upcoming Sunday. By the time we finished sharing our reflection on the Bible passage, it was clear to them that I was not there to judge them, but to facilitate a process for them to honestly look at themselves as a community that happened to have an exclusive reputation. At the end of that meeting, we contracted for a monthly meeting for the next five months.

For the next meeting, I plotted the congregation's average Sunday attendance statistics of the last fifteen years in a graphic chart. Fifteen years ago, the congregation was one hundred and fifty people strong. Five years later, the attendance suddenly dropped to seventy-five. In another five years, they were down to forty-five people. I also knew that their most recent pastors had all gone on stress leaves. After presenting the Sunday attendance chart, I asked them what had happened in the years when half the congregation left the church. I was challenging their explicit boundary function, which projected them as a loving, welcoming community. I was trying to help them reveal the implicit part of the boundary function—the part that is not readily apparent, conscious, or articulated. After a not-so-easy struggle, they finally revealed that they had an organist who was strongly biased toward a certain type of church music. Every time a person or group complained about the music, the organist would threaten to resign, and the church leaders would rally around her, begging her to come back. When she came back, she continued to do what she had always done with the music ministry, and the group that complained eventually left. This pattern repeated itself over the ensuing fifteen years. That was the *real* boundary function of this congregation: This organist was the gatekeeper.

Over the next five months, we used the same format each time we met: Respectful Communication Guidelines, Bible study, and then discussion of a specific topic. As part of their homework for one of the later meetings, the participants did a survey, asking the congregation to tell them what they liked about their worship services and how they could improve them. Two thirds of the congregation said in the survey that they would like more new music from the newly published denominational hymnal. The organist read the summary of the survey data and immediately threatened to resign; this time, however, the church committee recognized that the pattern was about to repeat itself. Instead of following the old pattern, members stepped out of their safe zone and wrote a letter of reply, saying that they wanted her to continue to be their organist but that they would like to have at least two new hymns on each Sunday. The response from the organist was, "I don't play that stuff." The church committee simply accepted her resignation.

Since then the congregation has hired a new organist, who has responded to the musical needs and interests of the congregation. They have started a newcomer program in which they deliver a basket of bread and other homemade goodies to the home of newcomers within the first week of their visit. The newcomers keep coming and staying. For the first time in fifteen years, the congregation is growing. The church committee took on the gatekeeper's responsibility and opened the gate for the Good Shepherd. They welcomed Christ into their midst, and Christ became their gate and let them out into the grace margin where they could become a truly welcoming community.

One of the most effective ways to help a community revisit its safe zone is to enable the community to honestly review its history. In this kind of process, we look for repeated patterns that might tell us something about the implicit boundary function of the community. As in the example above, based on a simple visual analysis of the Sunday attendance statistics, the congregation was confronted with the repeated pattern of half of the congregation leaving the church every five years. This pattern provided a jumping-off point for reflection and discovery.

Besides analyzing parish statistics, I have also successfully facilitated the following process, which can help a church community learn and affirm its history.

When facilitating a parish retreat or discovery day, I divide the members into decade groups. The people who joined the church in the 1930s form one group, the people who joined the church in the 1940s another group, and so on. Once they are in their groups, they are given the task of discussing and recording three strengths and three struggles that they faced in their decade. The groups then return and report to the large group. This activity helps the members of the congregation to recall their history as experienced and lived by them. Usually, at the end of the process the congregation regains a real sense of their heritage, their strengths, their identity, and their reason for existing over the years. At the same time, they may have discovered their weaknesses, struggles, and even patterns of exclusion. (See appendix C for a full description of the process.)

Here are two more examples of repeated patterns discovered by using the above process. After completing the history activity, congregation members discovered that every time they were faced with a challenge, instead of dealing with it directly, they would inevitably start a major building or renovation project. Avoiding the real issues had made the church building more beautiful, but this avoidance cost the church by continuing its decline in membership, while the remaining members' giving reached the breaking point. This pattern of avoidance protected the safe zone of the community. But if the community wanted to reverse its trend of decline, it would have to break this pattern of avoidance consciously and step out into the grace margin.

In another congregation, the community discovered, after dividing into the decade groups, that there were a large number of old-timers who had joined the church in the 1950s, but there were only two people who had joined in the 1960s, two in the 1970s, and three in the 1980s. Only in the 1990s did the number of joiners increase to fifteen. Meanwhile, further exploration had revealed that the major conflict of the congregation was between the 1950s group and the 1990s group. The pattern indicated that the 1950s group had consistently excluded newcomers from becoming members for thirty years. Their last pastor had been successful in bringing in new members in the 1990s but had not dealt with the exclusive boundary function of the 1950s group. Therefore, the 1990s newcomers were complaining about not being accepted as full members of the church.

A community cannot step out of its safe zone unless it knows what its safe zone boundary is and how it works. Again, we can only discern its existence by observing and recognizing repeated exclusive patterns.[1] In order for a community to truly enter into the grace margin, it must discover, acknowledge, and break out of its old exclusive pattern. A community must liberate itself from the bondage of its exclusive pattern to embrace the abundant grace of God.

---

[1]When dealing with racial and cultural issues, exclusive patterns of a community can be discerned from exploring the different forms of ethnocentrism. I have described in detail seven different forms of ethnocentrism in Eric H. F. Law, *The Bush Was Blazing but Not Consumed* (St. Louis: Chalice Press, 1996), 46–60. Helping a community to discern where the majority of its members are in this continuum will enable the community to determine its readiness to enter the inclusion process and which strategic programs it needs to provide its members to prepare them for entering into the grace margin.

Very often the gatekeepers of the safe zone are powerful, influential individuals in the community. Sometimes the gatekeeper may not be any one person or group of individuals. It may be something embedded in the structure or the organization of the community. Besides exploring a community's history, I also use processes that enable the community to analyze its present ministry and operating structure. The "three-legged stool" process, as we called it in the Diocese of New Westminster, is one that we have used successfully with many congregations. (See appendix D for the full description.) The process invites the congregation leaders to think of their church's ministry in three different components. For a congregation to exercise its ministries effectively, it must achieve a balance of the three components. Each component is like one of the legs of a three-legged stool. Each component must support the other two. If even one is short, the congregation's effectiveness as the body of Christ is diminished.

Here are descriptions of the three components:[2]

1. Ministry *of* the church is what the congregation does to manifest Christ to the world through serving the needy, proclaiming hope, working for peace and justice, and healing the sick in the large community and in the world.

2. Ministry *in* the church is what the congregation does to maintain, support, and develop the communities within the congregation and its physical resources.

3. Ministry *to* the church is the leadership structure that empowers the people of the congregation for ministry, according to their gifts.

After some questions and answers clarifying the three components, the congregation's members are divided into three groups according to their interests. Each group is asked to

---

[2]I am grateful to Graeme Nichols, who worked in the field of congregational development in New Zealand. While we were having a conversation about congregational development concerns a few years ago, he shared a similar process that he used with congregations in New Zealand. I have no idea how different or similar the process I am describing here is to his, but, nevertheless, I am thankful for process-oriented people like Graeme.

describe its component of the church's ministry in detail through listing the various individuals' and groups' ministries. If they wish, they can draw a pictorial representation. Each group is to report back. Then I facilitate a discussion on how each of the legs supports the other two.

Having done this process with at least twenty congregations, I discovered that the most revealing, but usually the most difficult, part of the process is the "ministry to the church" component. In exploring this component of ministry, the community usually reveals the structure of its boundary function, which may indicate to its members who and what the gatekeepers are in the community.

For example, St. Andrew's, which had been struggling with its inablility to grow beyond 175 members for the past five years, described its "ministry to the church" with concentric circles around the priest. Lines of communication moved from the edge of the circles to the center—the priest—forming a multipointed star. The priest, who requested my help, had expressed concerns that he was overworked, and he was a little frustrated that there were not enough volunteers to take up the various ministry tasks. He said, "Everything that happened that was new in the last three years had to be initiated by me and was eventually implemented by me."

After some discussion on how the "ministry to the church" supported or did not support the other two legs of ministries, I presented Arlin Rothauge's theory on congregation sizes.[3] Specifically, I focused on what Rothauge called "pastoral church" and "program church." In effect, the congregation described the operation of a pastoral church. In Rothauge's words,

In the pastoral church most newcomers find their ways into the membership circle through the pastoral work

[3]This material is from Arlin J. Rothauge, *Sizing Up a Congregation for New Member Ministry* (New York: The Domestic and Foreign Missionary Society, 1995). This booklet is part one of a five-part Congregational Vitality series. I found the analysis and description of all the different congregation sizes—family, pastoral, program, and corporate sizes—to be very helpful to congregations striving to understand their organizational patterns.

of the clergyperson. In this type of church, few visitors stay who cannot relate to the priest-in-charge…The membership looks first to the central leader for direction, inspiration, and pastoral care…If the congregation becomes larger in size, the internal dynamics will change because it will no longer be possible to operate as a super-family with a "big daddy."[4]

According to Rothauge, a typical functional size of this type of church is between 50 and 150 active attending members. No wonder the priest at St. Andrew's was experiencing stress. The congregation had grown beyond what the existing boundary function—that of a pastoral church—could accommodate.

After the congregation leaders acknowledged the weakness of their boundary function, I presented the structure and function of the 150–350 member congregation, the "program church," and what they needed to do in order to make the transition. If they wanted to grow, as they had said, they would have to step out of the safe zone of the pastoral structure into the grace margin to explore, discern, struggle, and consider moving toward a new way of being a church—less centered around the priest and more centered around programs and services led by lay leaders. As a result of this activity, St. Andrew's covenanted with the whole congregation to enter into a period of transitional exploration. St. Andrew's was a healthy congregation, and their intentional effort to move toward the new structure should enable the congregation to grow in the near future.

In this case, the gatekeeper was not so much an individual or a group of influential people in the community. Rather, it was the way in which the community was organized that limited its ability to include more people. In other words, the gate of the community was too small to include more people who were interested in becoming part of the community.

---

[4]Rothauge, 16–17.

Helping the community understand its structural limitation will enable its members to decide whether they want to grow. If they do, they will need to consciously let go of the old structure and redefine and restructure the congregation into a new creation that can accommodate more people.

When we invite a community to revisit its safe zone with openness and honesty, the end result may be wonderfully surprising and can be the beginning of a grace-filled experience. First Church was an older community of people over sixty-five. The church was a historic building located on a hilltop of the town. In the last few years, many young families with children had settled in the town. The church members could see them on Main Street, at the movie house, in their supermarket, and in their schools. But the young families were not in the church. Some came to the church once but decided not to stay.

Puzzled and frustrated, the church engaged in a period of self-examination. In that self-examination, church members discovered that they might not be the friendly community they perceived themselves to be. When I asked them what they liked best about their church community and the way they worshiped, many of them said that they really liked the quiet, meditative atmosphere of the Sunday service. Someone then pointed out the incompatibility of wanting to have a quiet service and wanting to have families with children, because children always brought with them noise. Maybe a certain look at a couple with a noisy child conveyed the message that they were not welcome. They struggled with this dilemma for a while. Then someone said jokingly, but with an undercurrent of seriousness, "I don't know why we have worried so much about noise; most of us are half-deaf anyway." They laughed. What a relief it was for them to discover this simple fact.

With that insight, they were free to explore other ways of organizing Sunday worship. Before they made a decision, they spent some time listening to young families with children discuss their needs. They discovered that most young parents did not want to be separated from their children during church services. So having Sunday school for children in a separate room would also be a sign of unwelcomeness. The congregation decided to create a quiet play area at the back of the sanctuary with a quiet swing, crayons and paper, and other noiseless toys. When young families arrived, they could drop their children off at this play area, knowing that they would be safe with the adult helpers. While they were worshiping, they could also check their children periodically. This play area was also a visible sign, giving the message that children are welcomed in this church. This play area was the physical manifestation of the grace margin the congregation created to engage more fully the families with children. A month later, eighteen children and their parents came, then decided to return, and eventually became members of the church.

What First Church discovered as they revisited their safe zone was that their strength—their meditative worship style—became their weakness, and their weakness—their deafness that came with old age—became their strength. Entering the grace margin often has this effect. When we are faithful to God through Christ in our self-examination, we learn what Jesus meant when he said, "The last will be first, and the first will be last" (Mt. 20:16). We can comprehend what Jesus meant when he said, "All who exalt themselves will be humbled, and those who humble themselves will be exalted" (Lk. 14:11). We open the gate for Christ to enter. We let go of our control of the gate and let Christ be the gate. In our courage to examine ourselves and our community's exclusive pattern, we can die with Christ and rise with Christ in new life.

In general, a community's readiness to enter the inclusion process depends on how well it knows itself—its strengths, weaknesses, struggles, and threats. The greater its self-knowledge, the more readily the community can step out of its safe zone into the grace margin. Community leaders can increase the readiness of a community to act inclusively by providing the following disciplines:

1. Review the community history and learn from it on a regular basis, about every five years, using the tools described in this chapter.

2. Revisit the community mission statement annually to discern whether it is still relevant.

3. Analyze the community's existing ministry structure every three years or so to affirm the good ministry that is happening and facilitate restructuring or revising, if necessary.

9

Dancing in the Grace Margin

A First Nations[1] man named Fred had been attending
Sunday worship at St. David's church for more than two years.
He always sat on the last pew. Since St. David's had consciously
worked very hard at becoming an inclusive, multicultural community, the congregation's leaders could not understand why
Fred did not get more involved in the church's ministries. They
believed that for St. David's to be a truly multicultural community, a person with Fred's background should become one
of the visible leaders of the church. "We have all kinds of jobs
and opportunities, but he never volunteers," one congregational leader said. Another added, "We try to make all our
programs very culturally sensitive. We even started a series of
cultural celebration events in which we asked different cultural
groups in the congregation to share with us their cultures. We
were waiting for Fred to volunteer, but he never did."

In a cultural diversity training program, a team of leaders
from St. David's learned that their requirement for a potential
leader to volunteer was a boundary function unique to the

---

[1]"First Nations" is the term used in Canada to refer to people of native (aboriginal)
background.

North American European cultures. They learned that many people of other cultures have a different perception of power and authority.[2] Some people may require a direct invitation from the existing leaders to participate in the leadership circle of a community. They also learned that they needed to change the way they facilitated their cultural celebration events. In the past the cultural groups, without any specific instruction, would usually share something about their external cultures— food, songs, clothing, language, and so forth. Inevitably, they would conclude that they were really the same as everybody else in spite of their differences. Their underlying assumption was that dealing with difference was undesirable and should be minimized.[3] In the diversity training program, the congregation's leaders learned that for these cultural celebrations to have a positive effect in moving the community toward being more interculturally sensitive, they needed to teach the members of the community that differences among the cultural groups could be good and that learning these differences could help them become a stronger multicultural community. One of the techniques that they learned was to invite the different cultural groups to share how they were different from one another. In particular, they needed to encourage the various cultural groups to address this question: What are the unique things that others need to know about you in order for you to be included in the community?

With this knowledge, the pastor of the church personally invited Fred to come to the next cultural celebration event. He informed Fred that he could bring whatever and whomever he wanted to the celebration. As one of four different cultural groups featured that evening, he and his group would have twenty minutes to tell the gathering how they were different. On the evening of the cultural celebration, Fred arrived

---

[2]Eric H. F. Law, *The Wolf Shall Dwell with the Lamb* (St. Louis: Chalice Press, 1993), 13–27.
[3]Eric H. F. Law, *The Bush Was Blazing but Not Consumed* (St. Louis: Chalice Press, 1996), 56–59.

with a large group of people—friends and family members from his nation. They brought their drums and their traditional ceremonial garments. They sang; they danced the dance that only they could perform. Then they invited the rest of the congregation to join them in the dance that was appropriate for others to participate in. At the end of their sharing time, Fred stood up and said, "St. David's is our church."

St. David's covenanted with the whole community for a time and place to enter into the grace margin when it organized the cultural celebration. Having explored and understood their own boundary function, they consciously invited Fred to participate instead of waiting for him to volunteer. Furthermore, the leaders of the community used their power to shape the way in which the groups shared in the gathering, enabling the cultural groups to share how they were different. During the gathering, the insiders—those with the power—relinquished their control and gave the First Nation group the full power to present themselves. Reversing the power dynamics, the formerly powerful became passive listeners, and the formerly powerless became active speakers and leaders. When the First Nation group finished speaking, leading, and dancing, they sat down to listen and to learn from the other three groups how they were different.

In the grace margin, we invite the outsiders and the insiders to come together to share and listen to each other. In order to do that, we need to create an environment in which there is a symmetry[4] of authentic revelation, compassionate listening, and reciprocal exchange of power. Creating such an environment is not easy, because the power distribution is almost always uneven in this kind of gathering. The insiders are those with seniority, ownership, and control, while the outsiders are powerless, with no ownership or knowledge of the traditions and way things are done. The insiders are those who know,

---

[4]In Sara Lawrence-Lightfoot, *Respect—An Exploration* (Reading, Mass.: Perseus Books, 1999), the author consistently uses the word *symmetry* to describe the quality of respect between two persons.

consciously and unconsciously, the boundary function of the community, while the outsiders may have no idea about this function. It is very hard to maintain a symmetry of motivation to dialogue when the power inequality is always present, tinting every phase and coloring every action as a political power play.

The first key to facilitating the grace margin is to ensure that the parties involved do not enter the dialogue with legalistic and political motives. Instead, we need to redirect the encounter to focus on relational issues. We need to learn from Jesus, who spent his time focusing on the needs of the people whom he encountered. He saw hungry people. He saw people who had no shelter. He saw people who had no connection with God and with the world. He saw people who were deprived of the resources that God has abundantly provided. He had little patience for the power and legal games of the Pharisees and the scribes. He constantly pulled the legal and political maneuvers down to the ground level, where the needs of the people were acknowledged and met. He did not consider who had more power and influence before he acted. He did not ask whether something was legal before he did it. He invited people to withhold their judgment and to come down from their political towers and connect with others on the ground of compassion—to feel what others were feeling—and thereby respond to their needs, passions, pain, and struggles.

In the grace margin, we invite people to resist the legalistic and political approaches, which usually involve debate, voting, party politics, and so on. We do not ask, Who has the power and influence? or, Who is right or wrong? Instead, we ask, What are the needs and interests of the different persons and groups? We invite people to share their history, traditions, hopes, dreams, visions, beliefs, and myths. We ask them to explore and share the consequences of having these deeply held values—their strengths, weaknesses, challenges, and struggles. We ask them to share the stories of their community and describe their relationship with God. In the grace margin, we frame the questions in personal and relational terms. The following are helpful techniques:

1. Begin each gathering with prayers, songs, and activities that affirm the presence of God.

2. Present and discuss the Respectful Communication Guidelines at each gathering.

3. Study scriptures together using the Community Bible Study[5] method.

4. Carefully select topics and questions for sharing, making sure that the questions do not tend toward the legalistic and political, but focus on personal and relational concerns.

5. Frame every gathering in the context of a liturgy. For example, when I facilitate a day of workshop and dialogue, I often design the day as an extended eucharist. In the morning, we begin with prayers and songs. Then we listen to the appointed scriptural passages of the upcoming Sunday. Instead of a sermon, the participants share their reflections in small Bible study groups. Then we discuss or work on the first topic of exploration. At noon, we listen to the gospel passage again, and a preassigned person gives a short reflection. Then there is lunch. After lunch the group does more work on the same topic or on a different one. At around 3 p.m., someone leads the gathering in the prayers of the people. For the offertory, we offer the work of our day to God and ask for God's blessings. Then the table is set, and the bread and wine are brought up. A priest says the great thanksgiving and consecrates and breaks the bread. Communion is shared. The gathering is then commissioned to go forth to continue their work.

A second key to facilitating the grace margin is to maintain a symmetry of authentic revelation as we invite people to share from a personal and relational perspective. Sometimes, when one group is knowledgeable and willing to share but

---

[5]Law, *The Wolf Shall Dwell with the Lamb*, 121–31.

the other group is not ready, the sharing will be uneven, and as a result, those who are ready to share lose motivation in the dialogue. In order to reveal ourselves as a community, we must first know who we are. The step of revisiting the safe zone described in the previous chapter is crucial before a community enters into dialogue with outsiders. For the same reason, the outsiders must also have time and space to discern who they are and what their needs are before entering into the dialogue.

Furthermore, self-revelation requires a person or a community to be vulnerable. We invite people to show not only the exterior facts and figures about themselves but also their interior reality—their feelings, emotions, beliefs, values, patterns, and myths, which reveal who they really are from a deeper level. In doing so, we invite them to take the risk to be known and to be understood as who they really are, not who they would like others to see. With the power inequality embedded in these encounters, creating the safety for mutual revelation is difficult but essential. The first step is to create a trusting environment by helping the parties involved to understand clearly the meaning of keeping confidentiality. Then we must empower each group to articulate who they are by giving them tools to express themselves. We must also ensure that there will be empathetic listening. Besides the suggestions given in the last chapter, other techniques that are helpful are:

1. Intragroup preparation—give time for affinity groups to gather and discuss the concerns at hand before the dialogue event. Sometimes it is possible to incorporate the intragroup work in the agenda of the event.

2. Invite each person to commit to keep confidential any personal information that has been shared.

3. Provide group media[6] to enable each person or group to share not just with words but more holistically

---

[6]Law, *The Wolf Shall Dwell with the Lamb*, 89–98.

through images, writing, and other forms of nonverbal communication.

A third key to facilitating the grace margin is to maintain a symmetry of compassionate listening. As each group is invited to reveal itself to the other, we must enable the groups to listen compassionately—to put themselves in the others' shoes and to see, hear, and feel the world through the others' eyes, ears, and hearts. There is no communication if everyone is speaking at the same time; we simply have noise. Neither is there any communication if everyone is listening and no one is speaking; we have just a void. Creating an environment where there is a symmetry of power is not so much making sure that everyone has the same amount of power and influence at the same time. Rather, it involves more of a reciprocal exchange of power, functioning like a seesaw with dynamic movement. When one side is up, the other side is down. When one group is speaking, the other group is listening. Then the process reverses. The side that was down is now up and vice versa. The dynamic of giving and receiving, speaking and listening is what characterizes gracious interaction in the grace margin.

1. The Mutual Invitation[7] process, in which each person takes a turn speaking and inviting another to speak, is one of the most effective methods to facilitate the reciprocal exchange of power. Among other positive effects, the process enables the group to focus on each person as he or she shares.

2. Carefully arrange the agenda to give each group uninterrupted air time while inviting the others to listen empathetically. Sometimes eliciting feedback from the listeners to share what they have just heard without making judgment can reassure the speakers that they were listened to.

---

[7] Law, *The Wolf Shall Dwell with the Lamb*, 79–88.

3. Ask people to reflect on the question, What does it mean now that they have listened to one another? In what ways can they meet the needs and interests of each group while respecting each group's or person's values and beliefs?

In the revelation of ourselves, we also reveal our different relationships with God. We share the many faces of the one God. As we affirm the different concepts and images of God, which are all part of the one God, God is revealed more fully to us and we are more faithful. As we recognize the many dimensions of the Holy, we also see more clearly what is not of God. We become more aware of the idols that are all around us—the principalities and powers that claim to be gods. Principalities and powers such as racism, classism, sexism, and heterosexism seek to separate us from one another and from God. They try to deplete the abundance of God's grace, making us feel insecure and fearful of one another and pushing us to act destructively toward one another. In the grace margin, instead of allowing these principalities and powers to continue to divide us and make us act exclusively, we can name these creatures and expose them more fully so that we as a new community can work together to fight against their power and control. Not until the children of slaves and the children of slaveowners, the rich and the poor, the able and the disabled, the young and the old, men and women, and the gay and the straight can listen and understand one another's different experiences, can we comprehend fully the power of racism, classism, ableism, ageism, sexism, and heterosexism. Instead of fighting one another and making the others the enemies, which is what these "isms" want us to do, we surprise the principalities and powers by working together as a community of grace, trusting in God's abundance. In the grace margin, we tell of the mighty work of God through Christ, freeing us from the bondage of the principalities and powers.

As Fred invited the community of St. David's to dance with him and his group in the story I told at the beginning of the chapter, we too are invited to dance with the others, the strangers, the outsiders when we enter the grace margin. In the grace margin, we dance with one another, using a new choreography. In this dance, the choreography is quite different from conventional ballroom dancing, in which one partner leads all the time while the other follows. Christ is the choreographer, and he redefines the relationship among the dancers. Christ reorders our relationships with one another and with God. Each partner takes turns in leading, then following, and then leading again. In the grace margin, the first shall be last and the last shall be first. Those who think they know are those who are ignorant. Those who are humble are exalted. In the grace margin, the wolf shall dwell with the lamb, and no one will be hurt. For the grace margin is as full of the knowledge of God as the waters cover the sea. In the grace margin, we invite one another to come down from our ethnocentric tower of Babel and struggle with communicating our differences in different languages. In the grace margin, we take off our shoes and dance with the burning bush that is blazing but not consumed, thereby seeing that we can address hot, emotional topics without consuming one another. In the grace margin, we dance the dance of Pentecost, where the miracle of the tongue and the miracle of the ear came together to enable us to become a new community in which the mighty work of God is proclaimed.[8]

So then, putting away falsehood, let all of us speak the truth to our neighbors, for we are members of one another. Be angry but do not sin; do not let the sun go down on your anger, and do not make room for the devil...Let no evil talk come out of your mouths, but only what is useful for building up, as there is need, so that your words may give *grace* to those who hear...Put away from you all bitterness and wrath and anger and

---

[8]The images presented in this paragraph are also in Law, *The Wolf Shall Dwell with the Lamb* and *The Bush Was Blazing but Not Consumed*. Both books presented the theology, techniques, and processes needed to facilitate the grace margin.

wrangling and slander, together with all malice, and be kind to one another, tenderhearted, forgiving one another, as God in Christ has forgiven you. Therefore be imitators of God, as beloved children, and live in love, as Christ loved us and gave himself up for us, a fragrant offering and sacrifice to God.

Ephesians 4:25—5:2

10

Adoption, Exile, and a New Creation

The gospel according to Matthew begins with "the genealogy of Jesus the Messiah, the son of David, the son of Abraham" (Mt. 1:1). In this litany of male-dominated names, it is peculiar to end the genealogy with "Joseph the husband of Mary, of whom Jesus was born, who is called the Messiah" (Mt. 1:16). We know that there was no direct relation between Joseph and Jesus except through Joseph's marriage to Mary. Joseph was only an adopted father. Although Matthew raises up the bloodline as primary to Jesus' royal descent, connecting him with King David in the beginning of this genealogy, there is actually no direct connection at the end. This peculiar opening to the story of Christ points out that Christianity began on the concept of adoption rather than on ethnic or racial blood relations. Adoption—to include someone who has no relation to you and make that person a full member of the family—is at the heart of the Christian inclusion process.

To gain a deeper understanding of the Christian inclusion process from an insider's perspective, we must further examine Joseph's experience in the story of the birth of Jesus, because Joseph represented the established Jewish community of his time, with all the right connections. Matthew, the gospel writer, knew this and graciously provided us with a narrative written from Joseph's point of view.

> Now the birth of Jesus the Messiah took place in this way. When his mother Mary had been engaged to Joseph, but before they lived together, she was found to be with child from the Holy Spirit. Her husband Joseph, being a righteous man and unwilling to expose her to public disgrace, planned to dismiss her quietly.
>
> *Matthew 1:18–19*

Up to this point in the story, Joseph was doing all the proper and reasonable things in such a situation. Mary, as far as Joseph was concerned, was a woman with an illegitimate child. According to Jewish tradition, her future was doomed to be one of much hardship and rejection. Joseph was going to soften the blow, acting as a righteous and reasonable man, by dismissing her quietly. If he had done so, he would probably have married another woman with a good reputation, have had ordinary children, and have lived a comfortable life, fully participating in part of a society that would have accepted him and his family. But divine intervention changed everything.

> Just when he had resolved to do this, an angel of the Lord appeared to him in a dream and said, "Joseph, son of David, do not be afraid to take Mary as your wife, for the child conceived in her is from the Holy Spirit. She will bear a son, and you are to name him Jesus, for he will save his people from their sins"…When Joseph awoke from sleep, he did as the angel of the Lord commanded him; he took her as his wife, but had no marital relations with her until she had borne a son; and he named him Jesus.
>
> *Matthew 1:20–25*

I would like to think that Joseph's inclusion of Mary, who was pregnant with a child that was not his, was more than just obeying God's command. He might have been moved by his own compassion and love for Mary, knowing what she would face if he dismissed her. He might have acted according to his own sense of justice, knowing how his community would deal unjustly with a woman with a questionable reputation. His inclusion of Mary upsets the equilibrium of the cultural norms of his time. His courageous act of inclusion probably put him in a very difficult situation—perhaps to be laughed at or to be talked about behind his back. His willingness to accept the unacceptable allowed an opening for the new creation to emerge. Christian history began with Joseph's inclusion of Mary and the adoption of Jesus. To make room for someone who was considered unfit and outcast was to make room for grace. Mary might have given birth to Jesus, but the groaning of this new creation was found not only in her birth pains but also in the groaning of Joseph's facing a society that looked askance at him.

> An angel of the Lord appeared to Joseph in a dream and said, "Get up, take the child and his mother, and flee to Egypt, and remain there until I tell you; for Herod is about to search for the child, to destroy him." Then Joseph got up, took the child and his mother by night, and went to Egypt, and remained there until the death of Herod. This is to fulfill what had been spoken by the Lord through the prophet, "Out of Egypt I have called my son."
>
> *Matthew 2:13–15*

For Joseph, the consequence of adopting Jesus was to be driven into exile. Notice how the pattern of this story parallels the story of another Joseph in the Hebrew Scriptures—Joseph, the son of Jacob, who was betrayed by his brothers and sold into Egypt as a slave. (In Matthew's genealogy, Jacob was also the name of the father of Joseph, the adopted father of Jesus.) It was in Egypt that the Israelites were enslaved. And it was from Egypt that God, through Moses, delivered the Israelites into freedom. The exile into Egypt of the Holy Family, led by Joseph, symbolically pointed out the significant role that Jesus played in the reinterpretation of the exodus story. Jesus, the adopted son of Joseph, would enable the people of Israel to revisit and reinterpret their covenant with God with a deeper, renewed understanding.

> When Herod died, an angel of the Lord suddenly appeared in a dream to Joseph in Egypt and said, "Get up, take the child and his mother, and go to the land of Israel, for those who were seeking the child's life are dead." Then Joseph got up, took the child and his mother, and went to the land of Israel. But when he heard that Archelaus was ruling over Judea in place of his father Herod, he was afraid to go there. And after being warned in a dream, he went away to the district of Galilee. There he made his home in a town called Nazareth, so that what had been spoken through the prophets might be fulfilled, "He will be called a Nazorean."
>
> *Matthew 2:19–23*

When it was time to return, Joseph did not go home to Judea but settled in the district of Galilee—an area on the margin of the land of Israel. In the margin, Joseph and Mary nurtured, taught, and raised Jesus, waiting for the acceptable time to reenter Jerusalem, to reinterpret salvation, and to fully transform the community of God into a new creation.

Joseph's adoption of Jesus represents the initial expression and living out of the grace that Christ's ministry actualized. In the most personal way, Joseph stretched the narrow and tight boundary of his community to create a small opening so that Mary and Jesus could survive. He made room for grace. If we are to understand and live out the inclusion process, we must learn from Joseph, who calls us to stretch the boundaries of our communities by adopting and nurturing those who are considered outcasts and undesirable. In every age, there are individuals and groups, usually minorities, who are discriminated against and consistently put into a disadvantaged position. In every age, the people of God must have the courage, as Joseph did, to adopt the excluded. In that adoption, we move with the excluded into exile. In that exile experience, we discover the presence of God, renewing our faith and our understanding of God's salvation history in our present context. When we embrace the exile, we relive and reinterpret the meaning of our own liberation from bondage. When we return, we gain new insights into our reason to exist. We reaffirm our living, dynamic covenant with God. We gain renewed energy for Christ's ministry of compassion and justice. When we emerge from the grace margin, we give birth to a new creation.

St. John's had been in decline for more than five years. The congregation consisted mostly of English-speaking people of European background. The average age of the parishioners was around fifty-five and increasing each year. Financially, the church could only afford a half-time pastor. The neighborhood around the church had been changing over the years, and the majority of those moving into the neighborhood were of Asian backgrounds. After much self-reflection under the leadership of an interim pastor, the congregation decided that it wanted to reach out to include the Asian communities but realized that members had neither the resources nor the skills to do so themselves. The members adopted a plan to dialogue with All Saints' Church, a nearby congregation from the same denomination whose members were of a particular Asian background, and to explore the possibility of merging. All Saints', on the other hand, was growing beyond the capacity of its small church building and was searching for a larger space in which to relocate.

On a conceptual level, this plan made a great deal of sense. St. John's would get out of its financial difficulty. The congregation could be a good steward of its physical resources, using them to reach out to the population in their neighborhood.

And also, All Saints' would find a bigger space—the property of St. John's—in which it could expand. Instead of rushing into the legal amalgamation of the two, they agreed to contract with each other for a grace period in which to dialogue and explore this possibility in more depth.

Over a period of six months, leaders from both churches listened to each other's needs, goals, and visions for their respective futures. The process was carefully planned out for each meeting, enabling both sides to speak honestly and listen openly. The dialogue process came to a screeching halt, however, over the issue of homosexuality. The leaders of All Saints' spoke strongly against the acceptance of homosexuals in their church, while the members of St. John's conveyed to the All Saints' group that they had always been open and accepting of gays and lesbians. It was becoming apparent that the leaders of All Saints' were not going to compromise on this issue. St. John's was faced with the decision of whether to continue the dialogue. If they merged with All Saints', they would lose not only their language and identity but also their sense of the community of God as they understood it. By this time, they had had many opportunities to reflect and articulate their identity, values, and beliefs. They realized that the other churches in their neighborhood were also conservative. If they "disappeared," there would be no moderate-to-liberal voice in that community. With that knowledge, they decided to call off the dialogue.

From the outset, the effort for inclusion was a failure. Indeed, the local denominational leaders were quite upset that the merging of the two congregations did not happen. But that perception was based on the assumption that inclusion only manifests itself in the physical inclusion of people and places. A more gracious inclusion process was taking place. The dialogue in the grace margin had allowed the two groups to clarify and articulate their boundaries and values, which resulted in a clearer understanding of each other. They decided that the best way for them to include each other was not to merge. If they had gone ahead with the merger, the people of St. John's would have been excluded in the long run. An overall examination of what happened after they called off the dialogue showed that the people of St. John's had learned to respect and include themselves. They also saw the importance of their inclusive presence in the large neighborhood in which they resided. St. John's enjoyed a growth in numbers soon after calling off the merger. In their words, "suddenly, single mothers, the poor, and gays and lesbians in the neighborhood are coming and staying." For the first time in many years, St. John's was retaining newcomers. With its newfound confidence, the congregation was ready to develop a multicultural ministry in the next two years on its own.

The story of St. John's and All Saints' points out that if we are faithful to the inclusion process, we do not condition the outcome. Neither church insisted that it would adopt the other at the end of the process. They did not give in to the political pressure from the denominational leaders, who really wanted this amalgamation to work. By remaining open, they allowed God, through the Holy Spirit, to lead them in unexpected directions. From the perspective of the leaders of All Saints', they decided to reaffirm their boundary on issues regarding gays and lesbians. For whatever reason, they were not willing to stretch their community boundary that far. However, they were confronted with the consequences of this tight boundary function. In a joint celebration with St. John's, they affirmed the learning they gained from the dialogue, and they parted with St. John's on very good terms, affirming their place in the wider scheme of God's ministry.

On the other hand, St. John's was a community that had committed time and energy to explore being inclusive of a major population. However, that was only the first step. In its initial effort, St. John's was still operating out of an attitude of scarcity. The congregation did not have enough financial re sources, and was afraid of dying—both of which motivated members to enter into the negotiations out of All Saints'. In their own words, "We were so busy surviving that we forgot to be faithful." When they had the courage to step out of their safe zone and embrace the exile through their dialogue with All Saints', they were able to relive and reinterpret the liberation of God. They gained a clearer vision of who they were and what their reason for being was—to be a moderately liberal community in the midst of a mostly conservative environment. When they emerged from the grace margin, they called off the merger. They were no longer afraid of dying. They affirmed the abundance of God's grace bestowed upon them and could offer the same to the neighborhood community. They clarified and redrew their boundary. They found themselves to be a gracious, welcoming community where the outcasts and excluded were adopted. They found themselves once again embracing the exile by living in the grace margin of the wider church community. In fact, they became a grace margin of the larger church in the midst of a diverse and changing neighborhood.

Returning to Egypt is a way of staying alive spiritually. There will always be strangers coming into our midst to challenge our comfortable boundaries. Like the scribes and the Pharisees, we have a tendency to be lazy and stay in our safe zone, applying the simple rules and our comfortable politics to keep us secure. When we choose to relive the exodus story, we step into the wilderness, which can be full of uncertainties and confusion. But with God's guidance and grace in transforming our wilderness into a grace margin, our groaning becomes the groaning for the birth of a new creation. In choosing to relive the exodus story and connect it with the new contexts in which we find ourselves, a new equilibrium emerges, and a new community with renewed mission is born.

Through many dangers, toils, and snares,

I have already come;

'Tis grace hath brought me safe thus far,

and grace will lead me home.

John Newton (1725–1807)

Epilogue

"Tell us, how will we know when we have become a more inclusive community? What will we be doing that's different from what we are doing now?" a church member asked me after I explained the process for exploring how to be more inclusive. I thought about it, knowing that these questions were not easy to answer in concrete terms. I finally said, "It depends. It's different for different groups. All I know is that if we are faithful to the inclusion process, God will transform us into a new creation that can express itself in many different ways."

Seeing the puzzled looks on church members' faces, I found myself telling the story of First Church on the hill (chapter 8) and how the older members expressed transformation physically in the creation of a quiet play area in back of the church as a sign of grace and welcome to the families with young children. I found myself telling the story of St. David's (chapter 9), whose members listened to Fred and his family and danced with them. I found myself telling the story of St. John's (chapter 10), in which the transformation was expressed in ways that even the congregation did not understand; all they knew was that an internal change in the attitude, outlook, and faith of the community occurred, and the outsiders responded to it by coming and staying.

As I told these stories, I realized that these congregations not only created plans but that also their plans were expressions of their experience of grace while they were going through the inclusion process. There was an internal transformation that took place when they emerged from the grace margin. This transformation came from their experiences of God's grace as they struggled to reveal themselves and listen to others and to God. As they embraced the cross and died to the old, rigid, and no longer relevant rules, they rose with Christ in the renewed dynamic covenant with God. Full of grace and hope, they found new life, new equilibrium in unexpected ways. Reliving Christ's death and resurrection became their source of strength and security as they adopted the strangers into their family of God. They found themselves taking part in the body of Christ. They became a living sacrament. They became an outward and visible sign of the invisible grace that they had experienced in the inclusion process. They became the living presence of grace.

Where is this transforming grace margin in your own life—in the way you deal with the different parts of yourself, especially those parts you dislike and want to reject? Where is the grace margin in your family life—in the way you relate to your spouse, children, parents, and relatives? Where is the grace margin in your workplace—in the way you relate to your peers, superiors, and subordinates? Where is the grace margin in your church community? Is there room for grace in the physical structure of your church, its architecture and use of space? Is there room for grace in the annual programming of your church community? Is there a grace margin in the gathering of all the different committees and groups—church council, choir, altar guild, men's group, women's group, financial group, youth group, elderly group, Bible study group? Where is the grace margin as your church community interfaces with the neighborhood? How can people in your neighborhood enter your community through your grace margin? How is your church community being a sign of grace in the neighborhood? Where in the diocesan, presbytery, and annual conference operational and organizational structure is the grace margin? What do you do to enable the people of God to experience grace when you assemble in synods, annual conference meetings, and conventions? How is the church a sign of grace and blessing among the nations of the world?

In a world where grace is hardly said before meals to give thanks to God, where "grace period" is a limited time we have to pay our monthly debts without penalty, where most differences and conflicts are handled through the graceless legal and political processes, and where fear of not having enough reigns and drives almost every business and personal transaction, the church must work tirelessly to make room for grace. The church must learn from Joseph and be courageous in adopting those who are excluded. When we extend our boundary to welcome "one of the least of these" who are members of God's family, we welcome Christ in our midst. When we accept the abundant love of God and have the courage to die to our fear and our desire to control, we let Christ be our gate. When we rise with Christ as a grace-filled new creation, we become the body of Christ. The church must make room for graceful dancing in our stiff and rigid society. The church must become the grace margin in a graceless world.

Checklist for Activating the Inclusion Process

1. Define the boundary challenge to your community.

2. How much time will you need to covenant with your community to address this boundary challenge using the inclusion process?

    How frequently should meetings be held? How long should they be?

3. What are some parameters for this covenanted time?

    What are the community values you will honor as you begin the process?

    What will you do?

    What will you not do?

    What is the behavioral covenant for the time you spend together?

4. Who are the influential persons in your community? What steps must you take to encourage the necessary persons/groups in the community to support this process?

5. What self-examination process will you need to follow to help your community understand its present boundary function? its strengths, weaknesses, opportunities, and threats?

   Survey?

   Exploration of the community history?

   Demographic study?

   Others?

6. What theological reflection/sharing will you do during this period of time?

What are some of the key images of God and Christ and theological concepts that you need to raise up, explore, and share with the community?

7. What liturgical design and practice will you use to frame the gatherings?

8. Based on your responses to the above questions, draw up a one- to two-page covenant that you will present to your community, inviting its members to participate in the process to address its boundary challenge.

Appendix B
Rights, Respect, and Responsibilities

A process to help community members arrive at a set of community principles that they can affirm and uphold to enhance their community life.

How to use this process

The following is a set of worksheets that participants will complete in a one- to two-hour period. The instructions are on the worksheets themselves. The facilitator needs only to guide the participants through the process.

RIGHTS

Webster's dictionary defines right *as "that which a person has a just claim to; power, privilege, etc. that belongs to a person by law, nature, or traditions."*

1. What are your rights as a member of this community? (Reflect on this on your own and write your ideas below.)

2. Move around the room and collect at least two different responses to question 1 from other participants and write them below:

3. Review your answers to questions 1 and 2. What are some concerns that you have regarding your rights and others' rights? (For example, potential conflicts, misinterpretation, dealing with controversy, etc.)

RESPECT

1. Complete the following sentence:

   I know I am respected when . . .

2. Move around the room and collect from others two responses that differ from yours.

   a. I know I am respected when . . .

   b. I know I am respected when . . .

3. Compare the three responses and reflect on the following:

   What are the reasons behind the different perceptions of respect?

RESPONSIBILITIES

1. What are your responsibilities in upholding your own rights in this community?

   One of your responsibilities to uphold your own rights is to communicate to others who you are and how you would like to be treated.

   a. What do others need to know about you for you to feel included?

   In what ways can you communicate this information to others in the community?

   b. What kind of support do you need to effectively communicate who you are and how you would like to be treated as a member of this community? (Support can come in the form of policy, support group, regular dialogue session, one-on-one sharing, etc.)

2. What are your responsibilities in upholding others' rights in this community?

    a. Review your learning from the discussions on rights and respect.

       What concrete behavior and attitude adjustments will you make in order to better respect others' rights?

    b. If you observed that someone's rights were not respected in this community, what would you do?

3. What are your responsibilities in enabling others in your community to better respect one another's rights?

Possible Community Covenant

1. Review the learning from this activity so far.

2. List three things that you would do to fulfill your responsibilities in respecting and upholding the rights of each person in this community.

   A.

   B.

   C.

3. List three things that you would NOT do to fulfill your responsibilities to respect and uphold the rights of each person in this community.

   A.

   B.

   C.

4. Submit your list to a central person in your community, who will collect and collate the information. The community will meet again to read and digest the complete list and arrive at a community covenant that everyone can agree to uphold.

APPENDIX C
Exploring the History of a Congregation

Objectives: To help participants affirm the history of their congregation and to review the strengths and struggles of the past

Type of Group: A group whose members are diverse in age and experience in the history of the congregation

Size of Group: Works best for large group—at least twenty people

Setting: A large room where participants can form small groups in different corners without disturbing the other groups. Otherwise, use a space with breakout rooms for the small groups.

Materials: Respectful Communication Guidelines, flipchart, paper, and markers

Time Required: one hour

How to Proceed:

1. Preparation:

   Put the following questions for discussion on the flipchart:

   What are the strengths of that decade for the congregation? (List at least three.)

   What are the struggles of that decade? (List at least three.)

2. Process:

A. Ask participants to raise their hands when you mention the decade in which they started worshiping at the church.

B. Divide participants into groups according to the decades in which they started worshiping at the church. If a particular decade's group is too small (fewer than three), combine it with another decade group.

C. Have each group discuss the following questions and record the results on a piece of flipchart paper prepared before the session:

What are the strengths of that decade for the congregation? (List at least three.)

What are the struggles of that decade? (List at least three.)

D. Gather all participants again. Invite each group to report, starting with the earliest decade.

E. Facilitate a general discussion and invite participants to share personal learning. Be observant of repeated patterns.

F.' To close the session, ask participants to offer a one-word description of each decade. Write down the words on each of the decade reports.

APPENDIX D
Is Your Church Ministry Balanced?
(The Three-legged Stool Process)

In order for a congregation to exercise its ministries effectively, it must achieve a balance of three components of ministry. Each component is like one of the legs of a three-legged stool. Each must support the other two. If any one of the components is short, the congregation's effectiveness as the body of Christ is diminished.

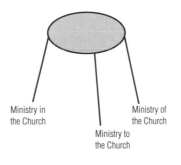

Ministry in
the Church

Ministry of
the Church

Ministry to
the Church

Ministry in the church is what the congregation does to maintain, support, and develop the communities within the congregation and its physical resources.

Ministry to the church is the leadership structure that empowers the people of the congregation for ministry, according to their gifts.

Ministry of the church is what the congregation does to manifest Christ to the world through serving the needy, proclaiming hope, working for peace and justice, and healing the sick in the larger community and in the world.

Instructions:

1. Read and discuss the information on this page. Make sure participants understand the basic concepts of the three ministry components. A good way to accomplish this is to invite them to give examples of each component.

2. Invite participants to move into three different groups according to their interests, knowledge, and roles in the community. Each group will discuss and explore one of the components.

   Group One:

   List the current programs, activities, groups, and work of individuals of your congregation that are part of the ministry *of* the church.

   Group Two:

   List the current programs, activities, groups, and work of individuals of your congregation that are part of the ministry *in* the church.

   Group Three:

   Draw a diagram representing the current leadership structure of your congregation.

3. Invite the groups to report back to the large group. Facilitate a discussion using the following questions:

A. In what ways does the ministry *in* your church support the ministry *of* your church?

B. In what ways does the ministry *in* your church support the ministry *to* your church?

C. In what ways does the ministry *to* your church support the ministry *of* your church?

D. In what ways does the ministry *to* your church support the ministry *in* your church?

E. In what ways does the ministry *of* your church support the ministry *in* your church?

F. In what ways does the ministry *of* your church support the ministry *to* your church?

4. Invite participants to reflect on the following questions and share.

   Having described and reflected upon the three areas of ministries of your church,

   A. What are the STRENGTHS of your church?

   B. What are the WEAKNESSES of your church?

   C. What are the OPPORTUNITIES for your church?

   D. What are the THREATS to your church?

5. If this is a visioning workshop, invite the participants to consider the following:

   Five years from now, what will the three ministry components of your church be like?

   a. Ministry *of* the church?

   b. Ministry *in* the church?

   c. Ministry *to* the church?